Pub 16.33

THE PHILOSOPHY OF JOHN DEWEY
A Critical Analysis

THE PHILOSOPHY OF JOHN DEWEY

A Critical Analysis

BY

W. T. FELDMAN, Ph. D.

GREENWOOD PRESS, PUBLISHERS
NEW YORK   1968

191.9
D519F
1968

PREFACE

John Dewey is the dominant figure in American philosophy today. A host of disciples look upon him as the great intellectual liberator of our times, for they believe that an initiation into the methods and principles which he has introduced dispels most of the plaguing problems which philosophers have heretofore felt themselves obliged to face. Once *das lösende Wort* is spoken, such typical issues as the " epistemological problem " and the " mind-body problem " drop away, for they owe their origin to a fundamental misconception of the meaning and function of knowledge.[1] Professor Dewey is great in the eyes of his followers because he has demonstrated precisely the manner in which the many generations of philosophers who have discussed these topics fell into error; and it is largely as a result of his analyses that the greater part of traditional philosophy is finally revealed as an elaborate art of self-deception—a quest for an illusory goal. No more serious indictment could be levelled against traditional philosophy, and if it is to survive it must withstand the attacks of Dewey and his school.

There are several possible methods of conducting an examination of Dewey's philosophy. The procedure to be followed in this volume is that of discriminating the premises, tacit or explicit, of his reasonings and the various motives which appear to have led him to adopt them. If this inquiry can be brought to a successful conclusion, the way will be cleared for an analysis of the arguments based upon these premises, and the worth of his philosophy as a whole can then be properly assessed. Some may object that a point of view is not amenable to argument, and this

[1] See, for example, James Harvey Robinson in *John Dewey, The Man and his Philosophy,* Harvard University Press, 1930, p. 160.

v

objection is pertinent if by a point of view is meant an
emotional or temperamental bias and nothing more. But
no serious philosophy was ever avowedly based upon an
emotional preference alone; and although the motivation
of a philosophical system may be emotional in origin—
a particular way of " feeling the push of the universe "—
what makes it a philosophy consists precisely in the *reasons* which are propounded to justify the specific emotional reaction.

If, then, Dewey's point of view is supported by arguments, they are open to scrutiny. It must not be assumed,
however, that the motives guiding a philosopher always
appear explicitly in his text. On the contrary, the manner
in which he attacks a given problem furnishes frequently
the best index to the considerations which are uppermost
in his mind. A study of Dewey's writings has convinced
the present writer that a number of quite distinct precon-
ceptions influence his argumentation upon philosophical
questions, and this study proposes to set forth these moti-
vating ideas and examine their interrelations. It should be
said at the outset that these leading principles are not all
of the same generic type; some are metaphysical, some
logical, and some extra-philosophical in origin. Nor are
they all coördinate; some are derivable either by logical
inference or by association of ideas from others. The
classification of them, therefore, can have neither strict
logical coherence nor mutual exclusiveness. Nevertheless,
such a study should serve two purposes: (1) by distinguishing the various points of view actually expressed or
implied by Dewey, it should represent the workings of his
mind more faithfully than an account which did not attempt this analytic dissection; (2) those interested in a
philosophy, not as the product of a particular mind, but
as a statement of a possibly valid doctrine about the

universe, should find such an enumeration of value. For if the various ingredients forming the given philosophical compound are analyzed out, the reader is not compelled to choose between a wholesale adoption or rejection of the system *in toto*. He is free to accept those doctrines which are sound and to reject the others. Thus many of Dewey's presuppositions appear to the present writer to be both true and important, while others seem faulty and untenable; both will be noted in their proper place.

What is here presented, then, is an enumeration and analysis of the principal presuppositions which have combined to form the basis of Dewey's philosophical position—the motivations which are chiefly operative in his thinking and direct his discussion of specific topics. The succeeding chapters take these up in turn and illustrate in detail how they pervade Dewey's philosophy. Their close interrelation will become increasingly apparent in the course of the exposition. At the same time it will be shown how, in the not infrequent cases in which these principles conflict *inter se,* Dewey is thereby prevented from expressing himself unequivocally upon specific issues, but must waver unceasingly between irreconcilable theses.

My debt to Professor Arthur O. Lovejoy is greater than any brief notice can express. This study originated at his suggestion as a doctoral dissertation, and his stimulating discussions and kindly encouragement are largely responsible for whatever merit it may possess. My first teacher in philosophy, Professor George Boas, has been helpful in many ways; and I should like also to thank those philosophers, too numerous to name, whose contributions to the journals have made less difficult the writing of this book. I wish especially to thank Mr. Arnold Frank, who suggested many valuable improvements in the manuscript, and Mr. Hyman Shapiro, who read the entire proof.

CONTENTS

CHAPTER I

THE CONCEPT OF ORGANISM

Monism, in one or another of its many manifestations, is a perennial philosophical doctrine. Upon certain minds, the belief that the Universe is, in some sense, One wields a potent and compelling influence. It is frequently assumed that the very existence of reason makes it necessary to conceive of the world as homogeneous and completely integrated. A century ago Hegel made a great contribution to philosophic thought when he discovered a path to this goal from what appeared to be an empirical point of departure. His examination of our actual concepts seemed to reveal the startling fact that they are all mutually interwoven and interdependent. Not only can no concept be thought of in isolation, but each also strictly implies every other as a part of its own meaning; and it proves, then, impossible to apprehend any portion of the logical structure without a conception of the all-embracing totality. This organismic logic was from the outset given a metaphysical interpretation, and the logical properties of concepts were accordingly transformed into attributes of the objective world. The outcome of this reasoning is obvious: reality becomes a logical system, every part of which owes its specific character to the position it occupies in the total structure. Thus even though Hegel's dialectic is now widely discredited, his system still commands respect as perhaps the boldest attempt at unification which the human mind has ever made.

At the turn of the century Hegel's supremacy was so little questioned in academic circles in America and Great Britain that his dogma of the essentiality of all relations found its way into the elementary text books of the day:

No phenomenon can be thoroughly understood in isolation, apart from all other phenomena. Strictly speaking, we cannot know one fact without knowing them all. ' To know one thing thoroughly,' as Professor James says, ' would be to know the whole universe. Mediately or immediately, that one thing is related to everything else; and to know all about it, all its relations need be known.' [1]

The same idea had earlier found poetic expression in Tennyson's familiar lines:

> Flower in the crannied wall,
> I pluck you out of the crannies,
> I hold you here, root and all, in my hand,
> Little flower—but *if* I could understand
> What you are, root and all, and all in all,
> I should know what God and man is.

In John Dewey's student days Absolute Idealism dominated the philosophy of both England and America. *The Journal of Speculative Philosophy*, established in 1867 by the Hegelian W. T. Harris, was the only philosophical periodical published in this country. In England, Green and the Cairds were at the height of their influence.[2] Dewey's teacher at the Johns Hopkins University, G. S. Morris, had studied in Germany in 1866-8, where he had become steeped in the Hegelian tradition. It need, then, occasion no surprise that Dewey should have felt intensely the Hegelian influence. In a recent paper he fully acknowledges this debt to the German thinker:

[1] F. Thilly, *Introduction to Ethics,* New York, Scribner's, 1904, p. 12. The author apparently treats as synonymous the innocuous remark that nothing can be understood in complete isolation from *everything* else and the entirely different statement that knowledge of one fact implies the knowledge of *all* others.

[2] Cf. J. H. Muirhead (ed.), *Contemporary British Philosophy,* New York, Macmillan, 1924, 1st series, pp. 309 ff., for a *résumé* of Hegelianism in England.

There were, however, also ' subjective ' reasons for the appeal that Hegel's thought made to me; it supplied a demand for unification that was doubtless an intense emotional craving, and yet was a hunger that only an intellectualized subject-matter could satisfy . . . Hegel's synthesis of subject and object, matter and spirit, the divine and the human, was, however, no mere intellectual formula; it operated as an immense release, a liberation.[3]

I should never think of ignoring, much less denying, . . . that acquaintance with Hegel has left a permanent deposit in my thinking.[4]

This chapter will be devoted, then, to an examination of the workings of the organismic logic in Dewey's thought. But, first, a possible misconception must be guarded against. It is possible to insist upon the Hegelian source of many of Dewey's ideas without denying or minimizing their points of divergence; for no matter how profoundly one philosopher is influenced by another, he may yet develop a doctrine so different from that of his master that the borrowed ideas are scarcely recognizable in their new context. Thus three successive stages of Dewey's thought manifest in distinctly different ways their common Hegelian background.

1. Dewey's first publications were plain expressions of orthodox Hegelianism. The following passages are typical:

[Psychology] is the ultimate science of reality, because it declares what experience in its totality is; it fixes the worth and meaning of its various elements by showing their development and place within this whole. It is, in short, *philosophic method*.[5]

Psychology . . . answers the question as to the significance of

[3] G. P. Adams and W. P. Montague (eds.), *Contemporary American Philosophy*, New York, Macmillan, 1930, II, 19.
[4] *Ibid.*, p. 21.
[5] " Psychology as Philosophic Method," *Mind*, XI (1886), 153.

the whole, by giving that whole, and at the same time gives the meaning of the parts and of their connexion by showing just their place within this whole.[6]

The very essence of psychology as method is that it treats of experience in its absolute totality, not setting up some one aspect of it to account for the whole, as, for example, our physical evolutionists do, nor yet attempting to determine its nature from something outside of and beyond itself, as, for example, our so-called empirical psychologists have done. The vice of the procedure of both is at bottom precisely the same—the abstracting of some one element from the organism which gives it meaning, and setting it up as absolute.[7]

This organismic logic is usually interpreted in a " totalistic " fashion. It is commonly assumed that the principle of the essentiality of relations implies that one must adopt the standpoint of the whole if he is to arrive at the truth about any part. The Absolute alone is genuine " reality," and is, therefore, the source and goal of all philosophic thought. To gain the universal point of view is, moreover, the height of ethical wisdom. The " totalist " minimizes the problem of human evil by contemplating the perfection of the Absolute, and he derives a vicarious satisfaction from the thought that he forms a part, no matter how fragmentary, of that perfect pattern. Consider the following passage from Royce's *Religious Aspect of Philosophy:*

Let us look away for a moment from our finite existence, with its doubts and its problems, to the conception of that infinite life. In that life is all truth, fully present in the unity of one eternal moment. The world is no mass of separate facts, stuck one to another in an external way, but, for the infinite, each fact is what it is only by reason of its place in the infinite unity. The world

[6] *Ibid.,* p. 157.
[7] *Ibid.,* p. 168.

of life is then what we desired it to be, an organic total; and the individual selves are drops in this ocean of the absolute truth.[8]

Grant this, and Royce's conclusion inevitably follows that "the one highest activity, in which all human activities were to join, is known to us now as the *progressive realization by men of the eternal life of an Infinite Spirit . . . Devote yourselves to losing your lives in the divine life.*"[9]

Dewey had already voiced the same thought:

God, as the perfect Personality or Will, is the only Reality, and the source of all activity. It is therefore the source of all activity of the individual personality. The Perfect Will is the motive, source, and realization of the life of the individual. He has renounced his own particular life as an unreality; he has asserted that the sole reality is the Universal Will, and in that reality all his actions take place.[10]

2. The totalist, in short, is primarily concerned with the nature of the Absolute; finite selves are dealt with only in so far as they require to be reconciled with it. In the 'nineties, however, as practical matters engrossed Dewey more and more, he was attracted to a different problem, and he began to develop his characteristic doctrine that philosophy should interest itself mainly with the rôle of reflective experience in human living. Radical as was this shift in Dewey's attitude toward philosophy and its problems, it did not involve a surrender of the old logical technique. The organismic dialectic remained as firmly intrenched in his thought as ever, but it now re-

---

[8] *Op. cit.*, Boston, Houghton, Mifflin, 1885, p. 441.

[9] *Ibid.*, pp. 441, 442.

[10] Quoted by G. H. Mead, "Philosophies of James, Royce and Dewey, etc.," in *International Journal of Ethics*, XL (1930), 227. Reprinted in *John Dewey—The Man and his Philosophy*, p. 100. This passage is said to be an excerpt from an essay of 1884, but I have been unable to verify the reference.

ceived a new interpretation which carried him far away from his original idealistic position.

Intelligence, Dewey observed, operates only in *particular* junctures of experience in which problems demanding decisive action arise. Centering his attention upon these special situations, he inferred their uniqueness from the principle of the essentiality of relations. Every juncture in concrete experience is essentially different from every other precisely because it is the product of a unique convergence and interplay of relations:

One who [believes that genesis of a thing in experience has nothing to do with the nature of the thing] is still at the static standpoint; he believes that things, that relations, have existence and significance apart from the particular conditions under which they come into experience, and apart from the special service rendered in those particular conditions.[11]

Interest in genesis . . . is interest in locating the exact and objective conditions under which a given fact appears, and *in relation to which accordingly it has its meaning.*[12]

Has the logician of a certain type arbitrarily made [the distinction between genesis and value] by taking his terms apart from reference to the specific occasions in which they arise and situations in which they function?   If the latter, then the very denial of historic relationship, the denial of the significance of historic method, is indicative of the unreal character of his own abstraction.   It means in effect that the affairs under consideration have been isolated from the conditions in which alone they have determinable meaning and assignable worth.[13]

In these passages are expressed two of Dewey's most

---

[11] *The Influence of Darwin on Philosophy*, New York, Holt, 1910, p. 260.

[12] *Ibid.*, p. 263.

[13] *Essays in Experimental Logic*, The University of Chicago Press, 1916, pp. 92-3.

distinctive contentions. First, constant stress is laid upon
the hazard involved in all intellectual activity. Just because the reflective agent is always finding himself in
" new " situations, he can never solve his present problems merely on the basis of general rules which have been
developed from past similar experiences. This argument
from " the uniqueness of every experienced situation " insists upon the provisional character of all general rules
and principles. Their applicability and adequacy must be
tested and retested, and no matter how successfully they
may stand up against the challenge of new circumstances,
they must be held only tentatively and subject to revision
or rejection, when they can no longer be made to fit the
facts.[14]

But unfortunately—as is frequently the case with
Dewey—a valuable insight becomes perverted into a paradox. Thus this moderate statement, which exemplifies
the true spirit of scientific caution as opposed to dogmatism and over-hasty generalization, is extended so as to
make all science impossible. You cannot meaningfully
speak of knowledge, as such, of a subject-matter, as such;
but only of knowledge of a subject-matter determined by
a unique problem. " Knowing," Dewey states, " always
has a *particular* purpose, and its solution must be a function of its conditions in connection with *additional* ones
which are brought to bear. Every reflective knowledge, in
other words, has a specific task which is set by a concrete
and empirical situation." [15] Every case of knowing is thus

---

[14] *The Influence of Darwin on Philosophy,* pp. 151-3. This strain in
Dewey has had its widest influence among workers in the social sciences
and in law. Provisionalism does not deny the utility or possibility of
formulating generalizations, but it merely requires that they be used with
caution. ·

[15] *Essays in Experimental Logic,* p. 12.

constituted by the conditions of its genesis and cannot be understood properly apart from its context. Knowledge as usually understood, *viz.,* a representation of a reality independent of and prior to the cognitive act, becomes an impossibility. Dewey's objection to the intellectualist " is not," he affirms, " so much the latter's emphasis upon logical factors in knowledge as his isolation of the knowledge standpoint (in procedure and criteria) from its functional place and rôle—an isolation which is equivalent, of course, to making knowledge an ultimate and all-inclusive philosophic criterion." [16] Metaphysics is therefore outlawed, since it attempts to arrive at a non-functional knowledge of reality unconditioned by any concrete practical problems of the knower or by any of his personal peculiarities. " Philosophy is itself a mode of knowing, and of knowing where reflective thinking is much in play. It is hence self-contradictory for an instrumental pragmatism to set up claims to supplying a metaphysics or ontology . . . [Instrumentalism] involves the doctrine that the origin, structure, and purpose of knowing are such as to render nugatory any wholesale inquiries into the nature of Being." [17]

Dewey's contention, reduced to its simple essentials, appears, then, to come to this: every instance of knowing has its own " perspective "; it is an outlook upon reality determined by the particular position and constitution of the knower, as he faces the particular concrete problem which at a given juncture confronts him. Any claim which knowledge may make to transcend the limitations of these individual perspectives is invalid. But this thesis, as the

[16] " Some Implications of Anti-Intellectualism," *Journal of Philosophy, etc.,* VII (1910), 478.

[17] *Ibid.,* p. 479. A part of this passage which echoes the Darwinian motivation is omitted. See below, p. 42.

slightest reflection shows, involves the weird paradox that common meanings and valid general statements are impossible. Not only would communication become inexplicable—since each individual occupies his own standpoint, and a given proposition would hence have a different meaning for each knower—but stability of meaning would also be impossible, even for an individual, since the factors determining his standpoint (his interests, purposes and needs) are constantly undergoing change. All reflective thinking would necessarily be ruled out of such a world, for such thinking must, by its very nature, be capable of referring to the same meaning no matter how variable the surrounding conditions. Although Dewey has not fully drawn these sceptical conclusions from his premises, they are immanent in his reasoning; and if they are false, the arguments upon which they are grounded must fall with them. We may conclude from all this that Dewey's dialectical condemnation of metaphysics and epistemology implicitly condemns at the same time all science, which is in its essence a quest for general conclusions which are intelligible and valid from all standpoints.[18]

3. By the end of the second decade of this century, Dewey's antipathy to metaphysics had noticeably weakened; in *Experience and Nature* his earlier position is definitely repudiated, and he admits unequivocally the validity of ontological speculation. But when Dewey ad-

---

[18] However, it must be said that Dewey expressly recognizes that stability of meaning is an actual fact. "Various persons talk about an object not physically present, and yet all get the same material of belief. The same person in different moments often refers to the same object or kind of objects. The sense experience, the physical conditions, the psychological conditions, vary, but the same meaning is conserved." *How We Think*, Boston, D. C. Heath, 1910, p. 125. It is a great pity that Dewey has not always realized the significance of these judicious words.

dresses himself to the main problem of that work, the
" detection and description of the generic traits of existence," he does not cast aside the organismic logic which
had so long been a part of his philosophic equipment, even
though—as we have just seen—it was one of the most significant contentions of his second period that this logic
rendered the very problems of metaphysics meaningless.
On the contrary, it plays a basic rôle in the formulation of
the new ontology; for the imprint of his earlier thinking
is clearly discernible in his discussion of his two chief
problems: the nature of existence as it is, in itself and for
itself; and the nature of existence as it is known.

(a) *The nature of existence as it is in itself:* Every
existent is particularized and constitutes a unique item in
nature.

All immediacy of existence has a certain ultimacy and finality, a
certain incommensurability and incommutability.[19]

Each [res] comes from something else and each when it comes
has its own initial, unpredictable, immediate qualities, and its
own similar terminal qualities.[20]

There is something unpredictable, spontaneous, unformulable and
ineffable found in any terminal object.[21]

Such immediate qualities as red and blue, sweet and sour, tone,
the pleasant and unpleasant, depend upon an extraordinary variety
and complexity of conditioning events; hence they are evanescent.
They are never exactly reduplicated, because the exact combination of events of which they are termini does not precisely recur.[22]

The persisting influence, in such passages, of the organismic logic should be obvious. Every existent is unique
because, by virtue of its specific locus in the total con-

---

[19] *Experience and Nature,* Chicago, Open Court, 1925, p. 112.
[20] *Ibid.,* p. 111.   [21] *Ibid.,* p. 117.   [22] *Ibid.,* p. 115.

figuration of nature, it is determined or mediated by a set of relations to other existents which cannot be duplicated. This does not mean, however, that these conditioning relations need be " given," for Dewey also holds that every event has an " immediate " aspect which is non-relational and self-contained. " In every event there is something obdurate, self-sufficient, wholly immediate, neither a relation nor an element in a relational whole, but terminal and exclusive." [23] And more picturesquely: " If existence in its immediacies could speak it would proclaim, ' I may *have* relatives but *I* am not related.' " [24] Although these passages may give trouble, they are not necessarily incompatible with those which asserted the dependence of quality upon relational sets, for their apparent inconsistency can be resolved in this fashion. Dewey presumably intends to maintain the position that existences are in mutual interaction and sustain relations among themselves which completely determine their nature, but that their relatedness does not exhaustively describe them since every existent possesses also an immediate aspect—what it is taken to be by itself—which is *also* qualitatively unique.

(b) *The nature of existence as it is known:* It is a major contention of Dewey's later work that knowledge explores the relationships of existents. It is not concerned with qualities because of their uniqueness and ineffability. Cognition deals with the " characters " of events, which are inherently relational; non-relational " essential properties " are a fiction of older theories of knowledge.

If knowledge is perception of relations, and if knowledge is to have to do with real natural existence, then Locke should have concluded that existence, as the subject-matter of knowledge, is

[23] *Ibid.*, p. 85.   [24] *Ibid.*, p. 87.

inherently relational . . . [Locke] retained the old notion of separate, independent substances, each of which has its own inner constitution or essence. Knowledge which grasps only relations—such as were the staple of the new physics—cannot grasp an inner essence, which remains accordingly hidden and mysterious.[25]

Similar expressions abound in *Experience and Nature:* " Everything that exists in as far as it is known and knowable is in interaction with other things. It is associated, as well as solitary, single." [26] " All this in effect is equivalent to seizing upon relations of events as the proper objects of knowledge." [27]

Knowledge and immediate experience thus supplement each other; the former reveals the interconnections of existence, the latter its qualitative uniqueness. Dewey's position is epitomized in the statement that " nature has both an irreducible, brute, unique ' itselfness ' in everything which exists and also a connection of each thing (which is just what *it* is) with other things such that without them it ' can neither be nor be conceived.' " [28]

There are, it would thus appear, striking similarities between Dewey's present metaphysical position and the one he championed over forty years ago. Then as now he argued that reality is an organic system of entities whose existence and character depend upon their interrelations with each other. However, his belief in our ability to apprehend this reality has altered strikingly during this

[25] *Philosophical Review*, XXXV (1926), 23. Dewey contends that Locke's relational treatment of knowledge involves the theory which has since been termed " objective relativism," but that Locke failed to arrive at this truth because he retained the conception of substances with inherent essences.

[26] *Experience and Nature*, p. 175.

[27] *Ibid.*, p. 264.

[28] *Journal of Philosophy*, XXIV (1927), 63.

period. Whereas in 1886 Dewey thought it possible to transcend the limitations of our individual standpoints and to attain in some measure the standpoint of the Absolute, he now infers from essentially the same premise that each of us is inevitably limited to his own particular perspective and that reality-from-a-perspective is all that can be known. " There are an indefinite multitude of heres, nows, and perspectives. As many as there are existences. To swallow them up in one all-embracing substance is, moreover, to make the latter unknowable; it is the logical premise of a complete agnosticism." [29]

This chapter does not pretend to contain all of the applications of the organismic logic to be found in Dewey's writings. We shall have occasion to illustrate this theme further in its connection with problems raised in subsequent chapters.[30] Sufficient examples have already been given to show its widespread ramifications in Dewey's thought and the tenacity with which he has held to it.

[29] The present temper of Dewey's thought is also much more realistic than it once was, for he has long since discarded the spiritualistic and mentalistic implications of the Idealism to which he was formerly attached.

[30] See below, pp. 19, 34, 63, 69, 108.

CHAPTER II

EMPIRICISM

Perhaps no period of philosophical reflection has witnessed so nearly universal an acceptance of a particular label as the current vogue of " empiricism " and the " empirical method." It is commonly assumed that the adoption of the empirical standpoint is the first step in the attainment of truth, and that " experience " can provide us with all of the material needed for our philosophical constructions. However, this piety towards a common formula (as is frequently the case in philosophy) does not imply an adherence to a common doctrine, for " empiricism " signifies, at most, an attitude rather than a specific philosophic belief. The hopeless ambiguity and confusion which infect the current use of the term " experience " render a philosophy grounded upon it necessarily vague and devoid of specific content; and the many diverse and incongruous doctrines which have been advanced by philosophers under this label lend color to the suspicion that its significance is predominantly emotional. Without attempting a general proof of this contention (which would take us too far afield from our main inquiry), the present chapter dealing with Dewey's use of the term will confirm it amply. A prominent feature of his thought is its aim to be empirical, and Dewey is typically modern both in his allegiance to " experience " and in his uncertainty as to what that term shall designate. Thus three distinct interpretations of " experience " are to be found in his writings: (1) In his earlier work it bears the traditional sense, as a succession of states of consciousness; and, moreover, all experience is cognitive.

(2) Experience is later defined in the terms of the biologist; it is the organism and its environment in mutual interaction. Consciousness is only a small and not a necessary part of it, and "knowledge" is a biological function developed in the struggle for existence. (3) A third view, "immediate empiricism," asserts that while all experience involves "givenness," it is *not* all cognitive. Knowledge involves reflection and the active manipulation of external objects, whereas "primary experience" is non-reflective and is the bare occurrence of qualitative immediacy. The sequel will elucidate these three conceptions and the different philosophical methods which are derived from them.

1. "*Experience*" *as consciousness:* An important offshoot of this doctrine is an idealism of a Berkeleian type. Such a philosophy asserts that experience is ubiquitous, that to exist is to be a datum of awareness, and that it is impossible to think of any existent which is not an object of knowledge. Passages such as the following are typical of the first stage of Dewey's thought:

Existence means existence for consciousness. . . . A known something . . . exists only for and within consciousness.[1]

How experience became we shall never find out, for the reason that experience always is. We shall never account for it by referring it to something else, for 'something else' always is only for and in experience.[2]

[The psychologist] must point out how consciousness differentiates itself so as to give rise to the existence within, that is, for itself of subject and object. This operation fixes the nature of the two (for they have no nature aside from their relation in consciousness), and at the same time explicates or develops the nature of consciousness itself.[3]

---

[1] "The Psychological Standpoint," *Mind*, XI (1886), 7.
[2] *Ibid.,* p. 9.   [3] *Ibid.,* p. 9.

Experience, then, is of the nature of consciousness. Dewey here but repeats the then current idealistic dogma that existence is an object of consciousness.[4] Empirical method is then outlined in these terms:

> The psychological standpoint is this: nothing shall be admitted into philosophy which does not show itself in experience, and its nature, that is its place in experience, shall be fixed by an account of the process of knowledge, by Psychology.[5]

This frequently marks the point of departure of a phenomenalistic or idealistic philosophy. However, from the standpoint of consciousness, there is only *one* experiencer. The *Erlebnisse* of another are never open to direct inspection, and the existence of other centers of experience is known, if at all, only through analogies and ·inferences from one's own data. Therefore, this philosophic method, when developed consistently, should imply solipsism. But the ultimate conclusion of this reasoning is even more extreme. For consciousness, as we know it, does not occur all at once but in discrete units: it is, in James's words, a series of " perches and flights." A whole-hearted " empiricism " would adopt the standpoint of one of these units, and consequently the totality of existence would reduce to the datum of one's present awareness. As Santayana has justly said, "any solipsism which is not a solipsism of the present moment is logically contemptible." [6] Dewey

---

[4] The revival of realism in this century, as is well known, had as an essential part of its program the refutation of this thesis. Cf. G. E. Moore, " The Refutation of Idealism," *Mind,* N. S., XII (1903), 433 ff., and R. B. Perry, " A Realistic Theory of Independence " in *The New Realism.* Perry's term " egocentric predicament " accomplished a good deal toward dispelling the fascination exercised by this view since it was first formulated by Berkeley.

[5] *Loc. cit.,* p. 3.

[6] *Scepticism and Animal Faith,* New York, Scribner's, 1923, p. 14. The fact that consciousness does not occur at large, that every case of

never drew these subjectivistic implications from his premises, however, because the logic of essential relations, as then construed by him, is "objectivistic" in import and transcends the standpoint of individual centers of consciousness. The combination of the organismic logic with this empiricism results paradoxically enough in the annihilation of the latter, for the outcome of their union is Absolute Idealism; and—whatever may be the arguments for the existence of the Absolute—it certainly is not experienced (in the sense defined), and its attributes are obviously inconsistent with such experience.

2. "*Experience*" *as the interaction of an organism with its environment:* A significantly different philosophy develops from the biological conception of experience which Dewey (as he himself tells us) derived from his reading of James's *Psychology*. Although several passages from that work [7] imply the indefeasible subjectivity of all experience, Dewey contends that there is another strain which "is objective, having its roots in a return to the earlier biological conception of the *psyche,* but a return possessed of a new force and value due to the immense progress made by biology since the time of Aristotle." [8] And he deplores the fact that philosophers have not yet adequately appreciated the enormous significance of this conception: "I doubt if we have as yet begun to realize all that is due to William James for the introduction and use of this idea . . . Anyway, it worked its way more and more into all my ideas and acted as a ferment to transform old beliefs." [9]

awareness is discrete and possesses a different date from every other, is usually overlooked by the would-be empiricist; and his failure to note this obvious consideration enables him to avoid the natural consequence of his method, momentary or instantaneous solipsism.

[7] E. g., *Psychology*, I, 226.

[8] *Contemporary American Philosophy*, II, 24.   [9] *Ibid.*

Dewey's altered conception of experience brought in its train extensive revisions elsewhere. The most outstanding of these is the relegation of consciousness to a minor rôle in the scheme of things. From a ubiquitous relation correlative with the whole of existence, it has shrunk to but one type of " natural event " among many:

'Consciousness ' . . . is only a very small and shifting portion of experience. In the experience . . . are all the physical features of the environment, extending out in space . . . and . . . time, and the habits and interests . . . of the organism. . . . When the word ' experience ' is employed in the text it means just such an immense and operative world of diverse and interacting elements.[10]

Experience is not identical with brain action; it is the entire organic agent-patient in all its interaction with the environment, natural and social . . . Experiencing is just certain modes of interaction, of correlation of natural objects among which the organism happens, so to say, to be one. It follows with equal force that experience means primarily not knowledge, but ways of doing and suffering.[11]

Dewey argues that his present use of this term, although unfamiliar in philosophy, is in conformity with common usage:

To a naïve spectator, the ordinary assumption that a thing is ' in ' experience only when it is an object of awareness (or even only when a perception) is nothing less than extraordinary. The self experiences whatever it undergoes, and there is no fact about life more assured or more tragic than that what we are aware of is determined by things that we are undergoing but of which we are not conscious and which we cannot be conscious of under the particular conditions.[12]

[10] Essays in Experimental Logic, pp. 6, 7.
[11] J. Dewey and others, Creative Intelligence, New York, Holt, 1917, pp. 36, 37. See also Influence of Darwin on Philosophy, p. 157.
[12] Essays in Experimental Logic, pp. 277-8.

He even goes so far as to deny that experience is private:

In first instance and intent, it is not exact nor relevant to say ' I experience ' or ' I think.' ' It ' experiences or is experienced, ' it ' thinks or is thought, is a juster phrase. Experience, a serial course of affairs with their own characteristic properties and relationships, occurs, happens, and is what it is. Among and within these occurrences, not outside of them nor underlying them, are those events which are denominated selves.[18]

Let Dewey call this an empiricism if he will, but we must insist that he accept the disabilities of his theory along with its advantages. If the guarantee of the validity of an existent is not its self-disclosure to awareness but its ability to play a " rôle in the executive order of nature," this empiricism is essentially realistic and open to the objections inhering in realism. Although Dewey admits that this conception of experience is useless for purposes of analysis [14]—because it is non-selective, and no criterion is furnished for determining whether a thing is or is not in experience—nevertheless, he attempts to derive from it a new philosophic method which is to take the totality of events as its starting point. A close scrutiny will reveal, however, that this is but our old acquaintance, the organismic logic, dressed out in a new terminology. Undiscriminated totality is lauded, while the products of reflection are relegated to an inferior status:

Experience is double-barrelled in that it recognizes in its primary integrity no division between act and material, subject and object, but contains them both in an unanalyzed totality. . . . Life denotes a function, a comprehensive activity, in which organism and environment are included. Only upon reflective analysis does it break up into external conditions—air breathed, food

[18] *Experience and Nature*, p. 232.
[14] *Ibid.*, p. 10.

taken, ground walked upon—and internal structures—lungs respiring, stomach digesting, legs walking.[15]

Empirical method alone takes this integrated unity as the starting point for philosophic thought. . . . Its problem is to note how and why the whole is distinguished into subject and object, nature and mental operations. Having done this, it is in a position to see *to what effect* the distinction is made; how the distinguished factors function in the further control and enrichment of the subject matters of crude but total experience. Non-empirical method starts with a reflective product as if it were the originally given.[16]

Dewey's reference to " primary integrity " and to the " originally given " shows clearly that he has not yet freed himself completely from the conception of experience as the conscious. A genuine conversion to the new point of view is incompatible with any bias for the given; for givenness, we were just told, is no essential characteristic of experience. We must conclude, then, that Dewey illicitly (if unintentionally) weights the scales in favor of the data of immediate experience at the expense of objects of cognition.

3. *Experience and Immediate Empiricism:* Thus far we have distinguished two diverse senses of " experience " as they have appeared in Dewey's writings. A third view sharing points in common with each of these remains to be discussed. It received its most extended elaboration in an essay of 1905, *The Postulate of Immediate Empiricism,*[17] but traces of it can be easily discerned in some of

[15] *Ibid.* (2nd ed.), pp. 8, 9.

[16] *Ibid.*, p. 9. If Dewey merely means that we start analyses with complex wholes, there is nothing new or startling in his view. It would seem, however, that he means more than this; apparently he thinks that there is something less real about elements and more real about wholes.

[17] *Influence of Darwin on Philosophy*, p. 226.

Dewey's most recent publications. This " novel philosophic method " was first formulated in these terms:

Immediate empiricism postulates that things—anything, everything, in the ordinary or non-technical use of the term ' thing '—are what they are experienced as. Hence, if one wishes to describe anything truly, his task is to tell what it is experienced as being.[18] The real significance [of immediatism] is that of a method of philosophical analysis. . . . If you wish to find out what subjective, objective, physical, mental, cosmic, psychic, cause, substance, purpose, activity, evil, being, quality—any philosophic term, in short—means, go to experience and see what the thing is experienced *as*.[19]

If our analysis has proved anything, it has shown that " going to experience " is not the simple and straightforward affair that Dewey's language suggests. It is evident that these statements have no determinate meaning unless the term " experience " can be made precise. The remainder of the essay throws light upon this problem, and the citations from it will establish that Dewey is, in effect, now advocating phenomenalism as the legitimate empirical philosophy—in spite of a verbal disclaimer of that doctrine.

I start and am flustered by a noise heard. Empirically, that noise *is* fearsome; it *really* is, not merely phenomenally or subjectively so. That *is what* it is experienced as being. But, when I experience the noise as a *known* thing, I find it to be innocent of harm. It is the tapping of a shade against the window, owing to movements of the wind. The experience has changed; that is, the thing experienced has changed—not that an unreality has given place to a reality, nor that some transcendental (unexperienced) Reality has changed, not that truth has changed, but just and only the concrete reality experienced has changed.[20]

[18] *Ibid.*, p. 227.   [19] *Ibid.*, p. 239.   [20] *Ibid.*, p. 230.

3

Since, according to this thesis, all experiences obviously involve awareness, it would be merely a reiteration of the first view discussed, were it not for the fact that it contains a new element in Dewey's altered conception of knowledge. Cognition is no longer mere " esthesis " or contemplative awareness, but the whole process of reflection. Furthermore, knowledge has no superior access to reality; indeed, Dewey tends, if anything, to subordinate it in this respect to non-reflective awareness. Thus in discussing the well-known Zöllner illusion, he says, " The lines of *that* experience *are* divergent; not merely *seem* so." [21] But nobody denies that the lines *as sensed* are divergent—else there would be no illusion; it is Dewey's refusal to recognize any criterion of existence other than givenness to awareness and his consequent failure to distinguish between appearance and reality which constitute the real stumbling-block to the acceptance of his theory. However, the motivation of his reasoning is intelligible enough, and it is impossible not to sympathize with it. Since he is particularly attuned to the qualitative richness and diversity of existence in its immediacies, he does not wish any of these characters to have their reality discredited by later reflective knowledge. He therefore attempts to construct a metaphysics which can do full justice to them. In the following passages from his most recent works, this position is restated. Dewey makes much of

those irreducible, infinitely plural, undefinable and indescribable qualities which a thing must *have* in order to be, and in order to be capable of becoming the subject of relations and a theme of discourse. . . . In every event there is something obdurate, self-sufficient, wholly immediate, neither a relation nor an element in a relational whole, but terminal and exclusive.[22]

[21] *Ibid.*, p. 235.　　　　[22] *Experience and Nature*, p. 85.

Empirically, things are poignant, tragic, beautiful, humorous, set-tled, disturbed, comfortable, annoying, barren, harsh, consoling, splendid, fearful; are such immediately and in their own right and behalf. If we take advantage of the word esthetic in a wider sense than that of application to the beautiful and ugly, esthetic quality, immediate, final or self-enclosed, indubitably characterizes natural situations as they empirically occur. These traits stand in themselves on precisely the same level as colors, sounds, qualities of contact, taste and smell.[23]

In itself, the object is just what it is experienced as being, hard, heavy, sweet, sonorous, agreeable or tedious and so on. But in being ' there ' these traits are effects, not causes.[24]

We experience things as they really are apart from knowing, and . . . knowledge is a mode of experiencing things which facilitates control of objects for purposes of non-cognitive experiences.[25]

From this derogation of the things we experience by way of love, desire, hope, fear, purpose and the traits characteristic of human individuality, we are saved by the realization of the purposefully instrumental and abstract character of objects of reflective know-ledge. One mode of experience is as real as any other.[26]

The purport of these passages is in the main clear, and they support the analysis given above. However, they are not entirely free from equivocation, for Dewey seems to be wavering between a whole-hearted phenomenalism, which treats the data of non-reflective experience as exclusively real, and " objective relativism," which attempts to cor-relate in one " objective natural order " both objects of reflective knowledge and " things " as disclosed to bare awareness.[27]

We may conclude, then, that Dewey succeeds in remain-

---

[23] *Ibid.*, p. 96.'
[24] *The Quest for Certainty,* New York, Minton, Balch, 1929, p. 131.
[25] *Ibid.*, p. 98.   [26] *Ibid.*, p. 219.   [27] See also below, pp. 55 ff.

ing empirical because he actually has two distinct concepts of experience. The " subjectivistic " type emphasizes the characters which are present in awareness, and which, Dewey agrees, are the effects of interactions of a vast number of external events. But this dependent event of awareness, in being immediate, is self-enclosed and does not refer to these external causes.[28] The " objectivistic " type performs a quite different function. It places the organism—upon which the existence of subjective experience depends—in a larger context of " doings and sufferings." Divorced from awareness, it becomes coextensive with the whole of nature—or, at least, that part of nature which causally interacts with organisms. Both " experiences " taken together furnish thus the basis for an adequate philosophy, since each tends to supplement the deficiencies of the other; but to call both by the same name can lead only to confusion and misunderstanding, and if either is taken as the foundation for an exclusive philosophic method, a one-sided and faulty construction must result.[29]

[28] See above, p. 11.
[29] The final chapter shows how incompatible these two conceptions really are when their implications are drawn.

CHAPTER III

TEMPORALISM

The eternal appears to have enjoyed a peculiar fascination for the metaphysically-minded members of the human species. Bertrand Russell once stated that "both in thought and in feeling, to realize the unimportance of time is the gate of wisdom "[1]; and though his remark is open to criticism as a statement of philosophic method, it sums up well the actual procedure of the great philosophers of the past.

Time is a feature of the world of our experience which has usually been treated with a sort of contempt by philosophy . . . ever since Plato's day. The speculative mind has been, by most of the great metaphysicians of the past, bidden to interest itself in the eternal and immutable. . . . In a hundred ways, older philosophies have shown that they were unable to make much sense, or find much of philosophic significance, in the queer fact that our world *is* a temporal one, that its contents come to us piecemeal, that a bit of experience scarcely *is* before it lapses into nonentity again, that all that we immediately *get* of existence happens in that infinitesimal bridge between an unrealized future and a derealized past, which we call the present moment.[2]

However, the present century, Professor Lovejoy continues, marks a widespread reaction against this tradition; and the practice of "treating time seriously" has daily grown more common. Several great figures in the philosophy of the present and recent past, James and Bergson, Whitehead and Alexander, have led this counter move-

[1] *Scientific Method in Philosophy*, Chicago, Open Court, 1914, p. 167.
[2] A. O. Lovejoy, "Bergson and Romantic Evolutionism," *University of California Chronicle*, XV (1913), 438. Any philosophy which neither denies the existence of time nor explains it away, he calls "temporalism."

ment which stresses the importance of time and temporal considerations for metaphysics. Similar ideas have influenced Dewey's philosophical development, and it is with the more important aspects of this influence that the present chapter will deal.

Dewey's temporalist strain can be traced to his first writings. It was an obvious corollary of his psychological standpoint and the "individualism" which it involved. Thus even while he was most certain of the truth of Absolute Idealism, he did not hesitate to say that "the universe except as realized in an individual has no existence." [3] Now the most characteristic trait of an individual's experience is its temporality. *Man's* experience is a succession of "presents," in each of which he is conscious of a "before" and "after" external to the duration he then occupies. The Absolute, indeed, was conceived as having the whole temporal series as its content in one luminous "moment" of awareness, but this, palpably, is not true of finite knowers. For them, at any rate, time considerations are of paramount importance. The Absolute, therefore, can be known only in so far as it is manifested in our finite consciousness. "For man, as object of his philosophy, this Absolute has existence only so far as it has manifested itself in his conscious experience." [4] "Dealing with an individualized universe, one of whose functions . . . *is* time, philosophy knows nothing about any consciousness which is out of relation to time." [5]

___

[3] "Psychology as Philosophic Method," *Mind*, XI (1886), 167.

[4] *Ibid.*, p. 164.

[5] *Ibid.*, p. 167. This is a somewhat extreme expression of a rather common characteristic of Hegelianism—the combination of a fundamentally eternalistic metaphysics with an especial preoccupation with the historic process. At that time Dewey attempted to reconcile the temporality of

Many years later a form of this temporalism served as the basis of an important conception in the philosophy of pragmatism, the doctrine that we live in an unfinished world, a "world in the making." [6] Dewey is tireless in insisting that the real is in a constant process of change, and he cites this in support of his hypothesis that knowledge transforms reality:

If one is already committed to a belief that Reality is neatly and finally tied up in a packet without loose ends, unfinished issues or new departures, one would object to knowledge making a difference just as one would object to any other impertinent obtruder. But if one believes that the world itself is in transformation, why should the notion that knowledge is the most important mode of its modification and the only organ of its guidance be *a priori* obnoxious? [7]

Other passages in the same essay have a similar import:

If things undergo change without thereby ceasing to be real . . . If all existences are in transition . . . If reality be itself in transition—and this doctrine originated not with the objectionable pragmatist but with the physicist and naturalist and moral historian—then . . .[8]

One set of considerations underlying Dewey's thought at this time (1907) is apparent from these quotations. Nature is fundamentally a process, a correlated series of events. To this conclusion Dewey is brought not only by

finite experience with the eternality of the Absolute by means of a modified Kantianism, but with the difficulties of that solution we are not concerned, for his subsequent abandonment of Absolutism renders the question of purely historical interest.

[6] James also argued effectively against the conception of a "block universe." See *A Pluralistic Universe*, London, Longmans, Green and Company, 1909.

[7] "Does Reality Possess Practical Character?" in *Essays in Honor of William James*, New York, Longmans, Green, 1908, pp. 56-7.

[8] *Ibid.*, p. 59. See also pp. 78-9.

the testimony of private experience but also by the procedure of the sciences. How, then, it may be asked, does
he show that change is not merely " phenomenal " but
also characterizes basic Reality? The proof of this theorem
is indirect, and consists in a demonstration of the untena-
bility of Absolutism; for it would appear that with that
doctrine discredited, some type of temporalistic metaphysics must be accepted.

1. *The practical argument against Absolutism:* Perhaps the most important single strain in Dewey's whole
philosophy is his belief in the effectiveness of reflective
thought.[9] But practical intelligence cannot function in the
block universe of the absolutist; it demands a world which
presents alternative options. Therefore,

A theory which ends by declaring that everything is, really and
eternally, thoroughly ideal and rational, cuts the nerve of the
specific demand and work of intelligence.[10]

A world already, in its intrinsic structure, dominated by thought is
not a world in which, save by contradiction of premises, thinking
has anything to do. . . . A doctrine which exalts thought in name
while ignoring its efficacy in fact (that is, its use in bettering life)
is a doctrine which cannot be entertained and taught without
serious peril.[11]

Dewey argues that an absolutistic metaphysics renders
meaningless the situations of doubt in which we, as
reflective agents, are constantly finding ourselves. To
avoid this result, the conception of a world in the making
is developed. In the felicitous metaphor of James:

On the pragmatist side we have only one edition of the universe,

[9] See below, Chapter VII.
[10] *Essays in Experimental Logic*, p. 22.
[11] *Creative Intelligence*, pp. 27-8.

unfinished, growing in all sorts of places, especially in the places where thinking beings are at work. On the rationalist side we have a universe in many editions, one real one, the infinite folio, or *édition de luxe*, eternally complete; and then the various finite editions, full of false readings, distorted and mutilated each in its own way.[12]

2. *The logical argument against Absolutism:* Absolutist philosophers are perhaps more than others content to rely wholly upon dialectic for the demonstration of the truth of their doctrine. Dewey turns their favorite weapon against them in the following passage, which contends that Absolutism is itself a self-refuting doctrine:

In the first place, the contents as well as the form of ultimate Absolute Experience are derived from and based upon the features of actual experience, the very experience which is then relegated to unreality by the supreme reality derived from its unreality. . . . If we start from the standpoint of the Absolute Experience thus reached, the contradiction is repeated from its side. Although absolute, eternal, all-comprehensive, and pervasively integrated into a whole so logically perfect that no separate patterns, to say nothing of seams and holes, can exist in it, it proceeds to play a tragic joke upon itself—for there is nothing else to be fooled— by appearing in a queer combination of rags and glittering gewgaws, in the garb of the temporal, partial and conflicting things, mental as well as physical, of ordinary experience.[13]

3. *The ethical argument against Absolutism:* Suppose Absolutism be accepted. What of it? In what way, asks Dewey, can it be relevant to the actualization of values in concrete human living?

[12] *Pragmatism*, New York, Longmans, Green, 1907, p. 259. James, in his usual conciliatory manner, attempted to reconcile the conflicting doctrines by giving a " pragmatic " meaning to the Absolute, but this met with small success.
[13] *Experience and Nature*, p. 61.

Is any value more concretely and securely in life than it was before? Does this perfect intelligence enable us to correct one single misstep, one paltry error, here and now? Does this perfect all-inclusive goodness serve to heal one disease? Does it rectify one transgression? Does it even give the slightest inkling of how to go to work at any of these things? No; it just tells you: Never mind, for they are already eternally corrected, eternally healed in the eternal consciousness which alone is really Real. Stop: there is one evil, one pain, which the doctrine mitigates—the hysteric sentimentalism which is troubled because the universe as a whole does not sustain good as a whole.[14]

This is an eloquent plea for the genuineness of transitory values and for their non-dependence upon any all-inclusive eternal absolute reality as the ultimate repository of value. Values come and go in human experience and are produced by human attitudes and human effort. If this thesis can be established, the ethico-religious demand for a transcendent non-temporal guarantor of values drops away, and the fluctuating, temporal flow of human experience can no longer, on that ground, be airily dismissed as " mere appearance."

Does the sum of Reality reduce, then, to the changing flux of things as presented in immediate experience; *i. e.,* is phenomenalism Dewey's alternative to Absolutism, or does the temporal flux contain within itself the elements of stability needed for the construction of a temporalistic metaphysics? Dewey's answer to this all-important question is not always clear, partly because of his equivocal attitude towards metaphysics, partly because of his failure

[14] *The Influence of Darwin on Philosophy*, p. 24. This passage appears in a dialogue " On Nature's Good," and these words are spoken by Eaton, the pragmatist, who is evidently the spokesman of the author. See the same volume, pp. 223-4, for a more formal expression of the same contention.

to draw the full implication of his temporalistic premise. In *Experience and Nature*, the outlines of such a metaphysics are presented. Experience is a component segment of nature, and its characters are assignable, by an assumption of continuity,[15] to the whole of nature. But the most distinctive feature of experience is its temporality:

The denotations that constitute experience point to history, to temporal process.[16]

Anything denoted is found to have temporal quality and reference; it has movement from and towards *within* it; it is marked by waxings and wanings. . . . Objects of present experience have the actuality of a temporal procession, and accordingly reflection may assign things an order of succession within something which non-reflectively exists and is had.[17]

Nature, which includes experience, must, therefore, be temporal also:

If we trust to the evidence of experienced things, these traits [the precarious and the assured, the incomplete and the finished, the repetitious and the varying, the safe and sane and the hazardous], and the modes and tempos of their interaction with each other, are fundamental features of natural existence.[18]

All existents are thus in constant "passage." Those apparently permanent are those which undergo change extremely slowly:

A thing may endure *secula seculorum* and yet not be everlasting; it will crumble before the gnawing tooth of time, as it exceeds a certain measure. Every existent is an event.[19]

[15] For Dewey's explicit assumption of this type of continuity, see *Experience and Nature* (2nd ed.), p. 28. An extended analysis of his use of this principle appears below, Chapter VIII.
[16] *Experience and Nature* (1st ed.), p. 28.
[17] *Ibid.*, pp. 29, 30.   [18] *Ibid.*, p. 75.   [19] *Ibid.*, p. 71.

Dewey, however, not only fails to elaborate the consequences of temporalism, but even goes so far, at times, as to deny its characteristic contentions, because of certain alleged disabilities which incurably infect human knowledge and render it incapable of representing the characters and relations of existences as they were prior to and apart from the act of knowing. He presents a variety of conflicting arguments, drawn from incongruous sources, in support of the doctrine that the object of knowledge is relative to the " perspective " of the knower: these four pertain to time or involve temporal considerations.[20]

(1) Dewey's antipathy to any philosophy which professes knowledge of " antecedent reality " is partly due to the accident that he takes this term over from traditional philosophy with its connotation of a transcendent realm of being, immutable, permanent and unaffected by the temporal process. Any " knowledge " which asserts acquaintance with a self-contained and changeless world of eternal essence is, to a philosopher convinced that the temporal is the characteristic feature of all existence, more than dubious. Dewey argues that a " spectator " theory of knowledge assumes the truth of some form of eternalistic metaphysics, and that since the latter is false, the former must also be false:

Knowledge . . . is thought [by the traditionalist] to be concerned with a region of being which is fixed in itself. . . . Being eternal and unalterable, human knowing is not to make any difference in it. . . . What is known, what is true for cognition, is what is real in being. The objects of knowledge form the standards of measures of the reality of all other objects of experience. . . . The idea is so familiar that we overlook the

[20] See also pp. 8, 40-2, 48 ff., 61 ff., 69-72, 94, for Dewey's other arguments bearing on this same question.

unexpressed premise upon which it rests, namely that only the completely fixed and unchanging can be real.[21]

Realistic, as well as idealistic, theories of knowledge, he charges, make the common assumption that

the operation of inquiry excludes any element of practical activity that enters into the construction of the object known. . . . The common essence of all these theories, in short, is that what is known is antecedent to the mental act of observation and inquiry, and is totally unaffected by these acts; otherwise it would not be fixed and unchangeable. This negative condition, that the processes of search, investigation, reflection, involved in knowledge relate to something having prior being, fixes once for all the main characters attributed to mind, and to the organs of knowing. They *must* be outside what is known, so as not to interact in any way with the object to be known.[22]

But the implicative proposition which Dewey sets up in this demonstration although correct is inconclusive. For— granting that an eternalistic metaphysics implies a spectator theory of knowledge—even if the premise is false, the conclusion may still be true; cognition can yield us an acquaintance with the veritable aspects of a changing universe. It is equally false to assert that the assumption that a fact is not changed *by being known* implies that the universe is itself not changing.

(2) Another consideration underlies Dewey's depreciation of knowledge as an instrument for acquainting us with the structure (or history) of existence. This pertains to the temporal position of the act of judgment. Dewey states that

[21] *The Quest for Certainty*, p. 21.
[22] *Ibid.*, pp. 22, 23.

The key to understanding the doctrine of the essays which are herewith reprinted lies in the passages regarding the temporal development of experience.[23]

Reflection in its distinctions and processes can be understood only when placed in its intermediate pivotal position—as a process of control, through reorganization, of material alogical in character.[24]

Reflection acts as a temporal link between two phases of existence to which knowledge is essentially irrelevant— the crude (sensory?) experience which raises the problem and the act (or acts) which bring the inquiry to a successful conclusion. Reality, as it is in itself, exists in a dimension incommensurable with the categories of mind; cognition reshapes reality, it does not mirror it. In short, a pragmatist version of Kant!

(3)   A third objection to the possibility of knowing the characters of a temporal universe is equally unconvincing, because it involves a synthesis of two incompatible principles: the indeterminacy of the future and the essentiality of relations. The argument takes the following form: In a temporalist's universe, the future must be in some sense novel; it cannot be a mere repetition of the past. But if the future is indeterminate, and if it and the past are so interdependent that neither can be adequately characterized apart from the other, then the past is equally indeterminate:

It may be contended that the past is over and its subject-matter all in and hence determinately fixed. . . . But the assertion that the future is wholly independent of the present is fatal to all intelligible discourse about existences having temporal quality. The belief that the past is merely past, that it is all ended and

[23] *Essays in Experimental Logic*, p. 1. The essays to which Dewey refers are those which first appeared in *The Studies in Logical Theory*.
[24] *Ibid.*, p. 19.

over with, rests upon precisely such an assumption of independence of present and future. The past, if taken to be complete in
itself, is arbitrarily sheared off from its future, which extends to
our present and its future.[25]

Nothing could illustrate better than this how foreign
to the true temporalistic thesis the organismic conception
really is.   For temporalism an event cannot receive its
character from what succeeds it.   There must be *some*
properties which make it what it distinctively is, so that
nothing which may happen subsequently, no matter how
intimately its existence is bound up with the occurrence
of the preceding event, can change the original character
of that event. Without this postulate events cannot retain
their individuality, and Reality becomes congealed into
a static system of internally related and *mutually* dependent entities.

(4)   There is also the familiar argument—at least as
old as Plato—which contrasts concepts with things-to-be-
known.   How can concepts which are static truly describe
existences which are fluid and changing?   A basin of
water, for example, is changing from hot to cold.   Therefore, Dewey says, it cannot be said to be either hot or
cold.   However, the situation, as the slightest reflection
shows, is still capable of being adequately described; for
in the first place, " hot " and " cold " are vague terms
which have no fixed range of application and should be
replaced by the more accurate thermometer reading; and,
secondly, a temporalistic theory makes all characteriza-
tions " respective " to time—it is meaningless to say that
an existent A has the characters X, Y, Z without signify-

[25] " The Sphere of Application of the Excluded Middle," *Journal of
Philosophy*, XXVI (1929), 703.

ing the date at which they are supposed to inhere in it
(some traits may, however, characterize the existent
throughout its history). Dewey is presumably committed
to the same position, and since the water has a determinate
temperature *at any moment,* his objection is without point.

It is because of the supposed force of these arguments
that Dewey hedges on the realistic and temporalistic posi-
tions which have been outlined earlier in this chapter.
There were, however, other motives in his philosophy
whose implications also converged to similar sceptical conclusions, and it is to a discussion of these that the three
succeeding chapters will be devoted.

CHAPTER IV

DARWINISM

Philosophers have always been prone to take over conceptions which have proved fruitful in science and to apply them in a substantially unmodified form to their wider field. It is not surprising, therefore, that Darwin's form of organic evolutionism found many philosophical counterparts soon after it was first formulated. The " evolutionary " ethics of the late nineteenth century and the philosophy of Nietzsche are perhaps two of the more notable of these. However, the most thoroughgoing application of the Darwinian hypothesis to epistemology is to be found in the writings of Dewey and the Chicago school of pragmatists.[1] It had for them a two-fold significance: on the positive side, it afforded a new " genetic " approach to the problem of knowledge which promised to produce a clearer and more fruitful conception of the way in which intelligence operates; and, negatively, it served as a premise in their attempted demonstration that the older lines of attack upon this problem—because of their improper orientation—are destined for failure.

The present chapter deals with this double influence of Darwinian biology upon Dewey's thought. He has acknowledged its far-reaching importance in many places, and chose as the title of one of his books *The Influence of Darwin on Philosophy and Other Essays*. Especially during the decade 1900-10 he believed that pragmatism was

---

[1] See T. and G. A. De Laguna, *Dogmatism and Evolution*, New York, 1910. As Professor C. W. Morris has pointed out in his recent book, *Six Theories of Mind*, pp. 278 ff., Darwinism had been employed as early as the 'seventies by Vaihinger, but its epistemological significance was comparatively restricted in his philosophy.

the Darwinian method transferred over into philosophy. The feature of the Darwinian thesis which is significant for philosophy Dewey sums up in these terms:

The significance of the evolutionary method in biological and social history is that every distinct organ, structure, or formation, every grouping of cells or elements, is to be treated as an instrument of adjustment or adaptation to a particular environing situation. Its meaning, its character, its force, is known when, and only when, it is considered as an arrangement for meeting the conditions involved in some specific situation.[2]

More generally, to understand the nature of any object, you must investigate the conditions of its genesis and the work which it accomplishes.[3] This analysis was then applied to the study of intelligence and knowledge. These are exemplified most strikingly in situations involving reflective thought, and for that reason much of Dewey's work centers about a discussion of such situations. That the *Studies in Logical Theory* (1902) is a Darwinian analysis is evident from the problems which are discussed: In what type of situation does thought arise? What is the particular stimulus to thought? What are the distinctions which arise in the reflective process? How does thought terminate?[4]

[2] Reprinted in *Essays in Experimental Logic*, p. 93.

[3] This "Darwinian" theory of "meaning" and of the function and consequently limited scope of knowledge is to be distinguished from a different application of Darwinism to epistemology—also called pragmatism—which sets up biological utility as the criterion of the truth of beliefs.

[4] According to this view "you are never to inquire what anything is, but only what it does, what its consequences are; pure descriptive analyses of temporal cross-sections of reality are to be avoided, and the character of any datum of experience at a given moment is always to be stated in terms of some other experience in which it is to eventuate." A. O. Lovejoy, "The Anomaly of Knowledge," *University of California Publications in*

We are further justified in terming this principle " Darwinism" since Dewey tends to describe in biological terms the context in which intelligence operates. He answers the questions propounded above as follows: Reflective thought arises only when habitual behavior is obstructed by a particular crisis in experience. In it the organism is confronted by divergent paths; the possible outcome of the situation is doubtful. The reflective agent must pause therefore to take thought in order to determine which factors are operative and how different courses of action will eventuate; he then chooses the solution which appears to be the most " satisfactory" under the circumstances. As soon as the problem is solved as well as the available data permit, he stops thinking and resumes habitual modes of conduct until another crisis arises:

Reflection . . . arises because of the appearance of incompatible factors within the empirical situation . . . [of doings, sufferings, etc.]: incompatible not in a mere structural or static sense, but in an active and progressive sense. Then opposed responses are provoked which cannot be taken simultaneously in overt action, and which accordingly can be dealt with, whether simultaneously or successively, only after they have been brought into a plan of organized action by means of analytic resolution and synthetic imaginative conspectus; in short, by means of being taken cognizance of. In other words, reflection appears as the dominant trait of a situation when there is something seriously the matter, some trouble, due to active discordance, dissentiency, conflict among the factors of a prior non-intellectual experience.[5]

Philosophy, IV (1923), 10. Although the value of the Darwinian analysis of knowledge is unquestionable, it cannot furnish a complete description of the phenomena involved in cognition.

[5] Essays in Experimental Logic, pp. 10-11. Compare C. S. Peirce, Chance, Love and Logic, New York, Harcourt, Brace, 1923, Chapters I and II: " The irritation of doubt causes a struggle to attain a state of belief. I shall term this struggle inquiry (p. 16). . . . Most frequently doubts

[Darwinism] intimates that thinking would not exist, and hence knowledge would not be found, in a world which presented no troubles or where there are no " problems of evil " ; and on the other hand that a reflective method is the only sure way of dealing with these troubles. . . . It intimates also that thinking and reflective knowledge are never . . . their own purpose nor justification, but that they pass naturally into a more direct and vital type of experience, whether technological or appreciative or social.[6]

Intelligence is therefore an instrument for the attainment of ends which are purely biological in character. An early study of this type of pragmatism so interpreted it and observed, as a fair implication of that doctrine, that " the whole utility—or, at least, the ultimate utility—of a newly arising function consists in its supplementation of previously existing functions, *in the accomplishment of previously existing ends.*" [7]

This study of the workings of intelligence bulked large with epistemological and metaphysical implications for Dewey. If, he argued, man is essentially an organism and cognition is merely an instrument to further activity, the

arise from some indecision, however momentary, in our action. Sometimes it is not so. . . . Feigned hesitancy, whether feigned for mere amusement or with a lofty purpose, plays a great part in the production of scientific inquiry (pp. 38, 39). . . . The essence of belief is the establishment of a habit" (p. 39). Dewey has also come round to the position that the doubt preceding inquiry may be feigned, in *The Quest for Certainty*. Cf. also *How We Think*, pp. 11-12.

[6] *Ibid.*, pp. 19-20. This passage was written in 1916 after Dewey's conception of intelligence had been subjected to criticism. I shall disregard for the present the last sentence in which he recognizes experiences which are " technological, appreciative or social " and limit non-reflective experience to purely biological functions. The remaining passages to be cited in this chapter justify this interpretation. Dewey's modified position which provides for the introduction of new ends will be discussed in Chapter VII.

[7] T. and G. A. De Laguna, *Dogmatism and Evolution*, p. 135.

traditional manner of conceiving knowledge and the rôle which it plays in nature must be invalid. Not only is there no reality which is not changeable by man's doings,[8] but also if there were such a realm it would be inherently inaccessible to human knowledge:

The organism has its appropriate functions. To maintain, to expand adequate functioning is its business. This functioning does not occur *in vacuo*. It involves co-operative and readjusted changes in the cosmic medium. Hence the appropriate subject-matter of awareness is not reality at large, a metaphysical heaven to be mimeographed at many removes upon a badly constructed mental carbon paper which yields at best only fragmentary, blurred, and erroneous copies. Its proper and legitimate object is that relationship of organism and environment in which functioning is most amply and effectively attained.[9]

Dewey performed an outstanding achievement, according to the late Professor Mead, when he freed knowledge from the supposed necessity of disclosing the characters of reality:

It is assumed that thought has the function not only of facilitating conduct but also of presenting reality as well. Even a theory of knowledge cannot serve two masters, and it was the task of freeing cognition from the shackles of a divided allegiance which Dewey accomplished in his *Essays in Experimental Logic*.[10]

This " new anti-intellectualism " Dewey ties up definitely with his biologico-social standpoint.

[It] starts from acts, functions, as primary data, functions both biological and social in character; from organic responses, adjustments. It treats the knowledge standpoint, in all its patterns,

---

[8] This involves an extension of the temporalistic thesis discussed in the preceding chapter.

[9] *Essays in Honor of William James*, p. 70.

[10] *John Dewey, The Man and his Philosophy*, p. 102.

structures, and purposes, as evolving out of, and operating in the interests of, the guidance and enrichment of these primary functions.[11]

Even though it may be true, he adds, that philosophy, as a mode of knowledge, renders things more intelligible and gives greater insight into existence,

these considerations are subject to the final criterion of what it means to acquire insight and to make things intelligible, i. e., namely, service of *special* purposes in behavior and limit by the *special* problems in which the need of insight arises.[12]

And, as we have already seen,[13] this essay concludes that it " is self-contradictory for an instrumental pragmatism to set up claims to supplying a metaphysics or ontology." It should be observed, however, that this conclusion follows only if Dewey is willing to assert the pragmatist paradox in its most aggravated form: *viz.,* that all statements must be translated into functional terms in order to express their " true meaning." [14] That he is at times so willing is already sufficiently apparent, but his contention is usually more sober. According to this more moderate view the words " intelligible " and " insight " are to be given their popular meaning, and " knowledge " signifies a mode of apprehension of the characters and relations of events; but Dewey adds the value judgment that such insight is of no intrinsic importance and that it only gains worth by the part it plays in solving the practical problems of concrete living. But this utilitarian depreciation of metaphysical speculation has no bearing upon the ques-

---

[11] *Journal of Philosophy, etc.,* VII (1910), 478.
[12] *Ibid.,* p. 479.
[13] See above, p. 8.
[14] See below, pp. 48 ff., for a discussion of this contention.

tion of its validity, and therefore affords no proof of its invalidity.

Before closing this discussion it may be noted that Dewey's infelicity of terminology in formulating his conception of intelligence and its work has left his views open to frequent misinterpretation. Thus, in the words of one lecturer, the new educational psychology has

disregarded the fact that intelligence long ago, perhaps scores of millennia ago, liberated itself to a great extent from the domination of the instincts (or what used to be called instincts) and began to ask questions quite outside the range of hunger and *libido,* to satisfy a curiosity not only about how to get food but about the "how" and "why" of everything, even about the useless "why": why the eclipse of the sun, why the family and state, why the stars, why evolution, why God.[15]

While it must be admitted that many of Dewey's expressions lend color to such an interpretation of his philosophy, the more liberal conception of intelligence which is to be considered in Chapter VII is more characteristic of his thought. It may be concluded, then, that Darwinism, in its strict sense, seldom had more than a limited application in Dewey's philosophy. He has employed it mainly for negative purposes, as a weapon against what he considered fruitless speculation in metaphysics and epistemology; and although it also served as a justification of his interest in his specific problem of knowledge, Dewey did not find it adequate for the development of his positive doctrine, and he was finally compelled to adopt a point of view radically inconsistent with that of orthodox Darwinism.[16]

[15] Tenney Frank, "The Log of the Pilot," *The University of California Chronicle,* XXXII (1930), 456.

[16] See below, Chapter VII. We have already seen in Chapter I how, in his third phase, Dewey surrendered the anti-intellectualism which he had earlier developed from his particularistic and Darwinian standpoint.

CHAPTER V

PRACTICALISM

It is hazardous to attempt to state any one element that is common to all the theories which have gone under the name of pragmatism. In its brief existence this term has been made to cover so many incongruous doctrines about meaning, truth and knowledge that an adequate discussion of its many vicissitudes is still in the future. Nevertheless, it is desirable to note the common motivation of these divergent philosophies—the belief that "theory" and "practice" are not separable and that theoretical considerations gain their intelligibility from the practical consequences to which they point.[1] This vague attitude may be termed "practicalism." It has an obvious affinity with the Darwinian strain in Dewey's thought, but is not reducible to nor dependent upon it. Dewey distinguished three problems to which the pragmatic method may be applied.[2] The formula which tells us to look "*towards last things, fruits, consequences, facts,*"[3] may be employed to determine either (1) our proper conception of *objects,* (2) the meaning of *ideas,* or (3) the value of *beliefs;* and the term "meaning" as applied to each of these has a different signification. Dewey discriminates his pragmatism from James's, because he is for the most part interested in the first two problems whereas James was more deeply concerned with the third. "If the pragmatic

---

[1] This statement as it stands is admittedly ambiguous, but it will serve as a preliminary formulation. The remainder of the chapter will be devoted to a clarification of it in so far as it is applicable to Dewey.

[2] In a review of James's *Pragmatism,* since reprinted as Chapter XII of the *Essays in Experimental Logic.*

[3] *Pragmatism,* p. 55.

44

method," he urged, " is not applied simply to tell the value of a belief or controversy, but to fix the meaning of the terms involved in the belief, resulting consequences would serve to constitute the entire meaning, intellectual as well as practical, of the terms." [4] A discussion of the pragmatic influence upon Dewey's theory of meaning naturally divides into two parts which are summed up in the conception of " the practical character of our ideas " and in the statement that " things are primarily denoted in their practical relationships." Both of these require detailed analysis in order to disclose their true significance.

I. *Practicalism applied to our ideas:* Some of Dewey's language, taken by itself, is quite extreme and seems to say that our only possible thought-content consists of ideas of those changes in objects to be brought about by our own activities. " The meaning of an idea is the changes it, as our attitude, effects in objects." [5] We are saved, however, from attributing this weird conception to Dewey, first, because " idea " in his terminology is restricted so as to denote only what may be formulated in a proposition; and, secondly, because the " meaning " of an idea—its reference to action—need not be direct or exclusive. It is, therefore, in his theory of the judgment that Dewey's conception of thought in its relation to action is developed most clearly. Does his discovery that judgment is conjoined with the solution of practical problems have any bearing on the meaning of such judgments? To Dewey's early answer in the affirmative, to his contention that all judgments refer directly to action, it was objected that judgments of fact do not satisfy this criterion, that they refer to a state of affairs whose char-

---

[4] *Essays in Experimental Logic,* p. 315.
[5] *Ibid.,* p. 310.

acter is definitely fixed and into which the judgments neither purport to nor actually do introduce any change. Later [6] Dewey attempts, while formally distinguishing judgments of fact from judgments of practice, to assimilate the former to the latter, and thus to establish, to some extent, the practical character of ideas. Into the success of this attempt we shall now inquire.

Judgments of practice are of the form " M. N. should do thus and so; it is better, wiser . . . etc., to act thus and so " [7]; and Dewey's analysis of them distinguishes these six traits: (1) their subject-matter is incomplete, for they imply that something must be done to complete the presented state of affairs; [8] (2) they select one of the alternatives to be acted upon and shape to that extent the future course of events; [9] (3) " the fortunes of an agent are implicated in the crisis " [10]; (4) the statements of fact which may be formulated during the course of inquiry " exist [only ?] for the sake of an intelligent determination of what is to be done " [11]; (5) these statements of the given are necessarily hypothetical since their pertinency to the problem at hand may always be questioned; [12] and finally (6) the truth or falsity of practical judgments is constituted by their outcome: " the event or issue of such action *is* the truth or falsity of the judgment." [13]

[6] *Essays in Experimental Logic,* pp. 335 ff.

[7] *Ibid.,* p. 335.

[8] *Ibid.,* p. 337.

[9] *Ibid.,* pp. 338-9. Throughout this discussion Dewey does not distinguish judgment from proposition. Chapter VII continues the discussion of these judgments in relation to the efficacy of intelligence.

[10] *Ibid.,* p. 340.

[11] *Ibid.,* p. 341.

[12] *Ibid.,* pp. 242-3. The " given " is evidently here used, not in the sense of the psychologically immediate, but as the definitely established or tested truth—analogous to the " given " in a geometrical demonstration.

[13] *Ibid.,* p. 346. Cf. also *Influence of Darwin on Philosophy,* pp. 148-

A detailed examination of this analysis need not be undertaken. Briefly, these so-called " judgments of practice " appear to be a complex type of judgment frequently found in ordinary non-technical thought. They are composed, as Dewey suggests, of two or more general hypothetical propositions of the " if—then " type, plus a value judgment: a singling out of one among them as describing the act which will prove most effective to the purpose in view. It must be noted, however, that the truth of *none* of the hypothetical propositions consists in, or depends upon, the performance of the condition, but upon the objective relations between the members of the pairs of events which are designated by the " if " and " then " clauses, respectively. *Which* consequent will follow is conditioned, it is true, by *which* antecedent is acted upon; but once a choice is made, the issue is no longer open; it is settled for all time by the logic of events. Nor can the truth of the practical judgment as a whole be verified by the upshot. For it acts as a *selective* agency; only one of the alternatives is realized, and, since the rest are thereby forever relegated to the limbo of unfulfilled possibilities, no sure method exists for determining the wisdom of the choice.[14] The verification of such a judgment must be, then, necessarily indirect and be based upon a comparison of its outcome with the issue of others arising out of similar situations.

Dewey is not content, however, to rest at this point and limit the scope of his analysis to practical judgments.

50, for an earlier discussion of judgments of practice, and *The Quest for Certainty*, p. 232, for a further development of the indeterminacy involved in these judgments.

[14] These points have been forcefully put by Professor Costello in the *Journal of Philosophy, etc.*, XVII (1920), 449.

He endeavors to extend his results to all types of judgments.   He asks:

How far is it possible and legitimate to extend or generalize the results reached to apply to all propositions of facts?   That is to say, is it possible and legitimate to treat all scientific or descriptive statements of matters of fact as implying indirectly if not directly, something to be done, future possibilties to be realized in action? [15]

Dewey does not develop this contention any further in that essay, but elsewhere among his writings arguments bearing upon it are propounded; and of these we shall consider, first, those appearing in his early essays and, second, those in *The Quest for Certainty.*

A. *The early essays:* Three types of arguments are advanced in support of Dewey's thesis:

(1)   The first of these repeats the genetic consideration with which we are already so familiar: the very existence of ideas is bound up with the practical needs of life.   If hesitation, uncertainty and doubt did not make living a hazardous undertaking, judgment and knowledge would not occur.

Will [the intellectualist] claim that without an original practical uneasiness introducing a practical aim of inquiry there must have been, whether or no, an idea?   Must the world for some purely intellectual reason be intellectually reduplicated? [16]

This point requires no discussion.   It is relevant to the origin of judgments, but it throws no light upon their " meaning," if meaning is equivalent to logical content. In short, the circumstances surrounding thought may tell us a great deal about its motivation, but they cannot

---

[15] *Essays in Experimental Logic,* p. 347.

[16] *Influence of Darwin on Philosophy,* p. 141. See also *How We Think,* p. 102.

prescribe the kinds of objects towards which it is capable of being directed.

(2) Dewey urges in a similar line of reasoning that consciousness is to be found only in problematic situations and that ideas are " problematic objects "[17]:

Where, and in so far as, there are unquestioned objects, there is no " consciousness." There are just things. When there is uncertainty, there are dubious, suspected objects—things hinted at, guessed at. Such objects have a distinct status, and it is the part of good sense to give them, as occupying that status, a distinct caption. " Consciousness " is a term often used for this purpose; and I see no objection to that term, *provided* it is recognized to mean such objects as are problematic, plus the fact that in their problematic character they may be used, as effectively as accredited objects, to direct observations and experiments which finally relieve the doubtful features of the situation.[18]

But this consideration is as little adapted to support Dewey's contention as the first. While it may be admitted that, in every referential situation,[19] our thought-content is dubious to the extent that we may be in error, this does not imply either (a) that these " doubtful objects " are surrogates for future experienced objects, or (b) that these are to be brought into the realm of the existent through action. Yet it is precisely these two questionable theses which Dewey wishes to maintain. But is it true

[17] By calling ideas " problematic objects " Dewey appears to be pre-judging the issue between psychophysical monism and dualism. This passage was written when he was rather favorably disposed towards phenomenalism.

[18] *Essays in Experimental Logic,* p. 225. See also *How We Think,* pp. 108 ff.

[19] The terms " reference," " referential situation," etc., as used here and in the next chapter, are borrowed from Professor Lovejoy. See his " Dualism and the Paradox of Reference," *Journal of Philosophy,* XXX (1933), 589 ff.

that uncertainty can be surmounted when, and only when, the object referred to presents itself *in propria persona* in future experience? And, further, by what license— except that of pure definition—is the term " idea " limited to signify those data which are employed as *instruments towards bringing into existence as direct objects of consciousness the things to which they refer?* This restriction is unwarranted by the quotation, for if idea is equivalent to what is given to " consciousness " (even in Dewey's sense of that term), it should designate, at the least, any present existent which refers to what is not then present. There is nothing more certain about our experience than that we frequently refer to objects which by their very nature can never be literally present in future experience. All such judgments—about our own past or about the experiences of others, can be verified only indirectly, by the presentation in future awareness of *other* " objects." I think, for example, of a letter which was to have been mailed to a friend, and I am not sure whether it was or not. The reference is to a state-of-affairs which is past and whose character is definitively fixed. No procedure is yet known for turning back the wheels of time to recapture that experience; the doubt can be resolved only by other acts of mine or by events which may happen without my intervention. Thus, if my friend replies to matter contained in the letter, my uncertainty will be at an end; yet this subsequent knowledge cannot alter the fact that the original reference was retrospective.[20]

[20] See Chapter VI for Dewey's futurism. He emphasizes here the practical character of the reference; *i. e.,* that the object referred to must not only be future, but also *receive in part its then character by reason of the present act of reference.* " Ideas are ' subjective ' . . . surrogates of public, cosmic things, which may be so manipulated and elaborated as

(3) Somewhat more happily conceived for Dewey's purpose than the considerations which have just been examined, is an argument which turns upon the following point:

As matter of fact, every perception and every idea is a sense of the bearings, use, and cause, of a thing. We do not really know a chair or have an idea of it by inventorying and enumerating its various isolated qualities, but only by bringing these qualities into connection with something else—the purpose which makes it a chair and not a table . . . A wagon is not perceived when all its parts are summed up; it is the characteristic connection of the parts which makes it a wagon. And these connections are not those of mere physical juxtaposition; they involve connection with the animals that draw it, the things that are carried on it, and so on.[21]

Here again Dewey calls attention to a fact which is frequently overlooked; namely, that many, and possibly most, of the common-sense objects of daily intercourse include as part of their definition a reference to human action and purposes. The full meaning of such terms as " table," " wagon," etc., is incomplete if their signification is restricted to those characteristics which are assumed to inhere in the loci which the objects themselves occupy; certain of their properties are " respective "—that is, they contain an implicit or explicit reference to a third term (either another object, a use or a purpose) to be determinable.[22] But when the meaning of this passage

to terminate in public things *which without them would not exist as empirical objects.*" *Essays in Experimental Logic,* p. 228. Italics mine. Although this may be admitted as regards some references, Dewey's extension of it to cover all is unjustified.

[21] *Democracy and Education,* New York, Macmillan, 1916, p. 168.

[22] This discussion is continued below, pp. 55 ff. The term " respectivity " has been recently coined by Professor A. O. Lovejoy, *The Revolt Against Dualism,* New York, W. W. Norton, 1930, p. 92.

is interpreted in the only sense in which it can serve Dewey's argument, it loses alike its value and its plausibility. The assertion that " every perception and every idea is a sense of the bearings, use, and cause of a thing " must imply that whenever we refer to an object—whether in perception or in thought—we must at the same time think of other objects or uses to which it may be related. As a psychological generalization, this is patently false; and, furthermore, it will be shown that certain classes of objects (those treated in the natural sciences) are definable without regard to any activity, and these are not covered adequately by Dewey's present discussion.

Therefore, while it may be freely admitted that no judgments are formulated unless there is a problem to be solved, and that ideas are " doubtful objects " (in the special sense noted), it by no means follows that the *kinds* of objects to which reference can legitimately be made are as limited as Dewey would have us believe or, indeed, that the mode of verification of such references is correctly stated by him.[28]

B. *The Quest for Certainty:* These arguments for practicalism have of late been powerfully reinforced by certain important new developments in the philosophy of science, and Dewey hastens to bolster up his case with this new evidence. I refer to the operational theory of meaning recently put forth by P. W. Bridgman, which,

[28] Professor C. W. Morris admits the realist's contention that " only that which is *explicitly* intended by the judgment is relevant to its truth or falsity " and that " instrumental guidance then becomes a judgment *about* ideas rather than the specific intent *of* every idea," and he quotes Dewey as saying that " were I writing afresh I fancy I should try to show that purely instrumental ideas are outside the province of truth and falsity—that is, as tools they are good or bad rather than true or false." *Six Theories of Mind*, pp. 311, 312. With this thesis the writer has no quarrel.

although it received its initial impetus from a limited branch of physics—the special theory of relativity—has been characterized by Dewey as "one of the three or four outstanding feats of intellectual history." [24] A theory for which such transcendent importance is claimed should be scrutinized meticulously to determine its precise meaning. In a passage which has been frequently quoted, Bridgman stated that "in general, we mean by any concept nothing more than a set of operations; *the concept is synonymous with the corresponding set of operations.*" [25] Dewey accepts this thesis and tries to show how operationalism is essentially identical with the doctrine for which he has been contending so many years. Thus in passage after passage he insistently asserts that all concepts refer to operations. A sample or two will suffice:

A definition of the nature of ideas in terms of operations to be performed and the test of the validity of the ideas by the *consequences* of these operations establishes connectivity within concrete experience.[26]

All conceptions, all intellectual descriptions, must be formulated in terms of operations, actual or imaginatively possible.[27]

Thought, our conceptions and ideas, are designations of operations to be performed or already performed.[28]

To judge that this object is sweet, that is, to refer the idea or meaning "sweet" to it without actually experiencing sweetness, is to predict that when it is tasted—that is, subjected to a specific operation—a certain consequence will ensue.[29]

Ideas are not statements of what is or has been, but of acts to be performed.[30]

[24] *The Quest for Certainty*, p. 114.
[25] *The Logic of Modern Physics*, New York, Macmillan, 1927, p. 5; quoted in *The Quest for Certainty*, p. 111.
[26] *The Quest for Certainty*, p. 114.
[27] *Ibid.*, p. 118. [29] *Ibid.*, p. 137.
[28] *Ibid.*, p. 137. [30] *Ibid.*, p. 138.

5

The parallel between these statements and Dewey's earlier utterances upon the subject of the practical character of ideas and knowledge is obvious. Does the introduction of the newer term "operations" bring with it any important modifications in his views? Analysis reveals that the same ambiguities which infected his use of the terms "practical" and "acts" are carried over to this more recent formulation of his position. Thus, in one passage, "operations" are said to be either "actual or imaginatively possible." But if this were the correct statement of his position, his theory would clearly fail to supply the restrictive criteria for meaningful thought which he obviously intends that it shall. For so long as thought concerns only operations, it *cannot* be otherwise limited or restricted. No one can think of any operation (not involving a formal self-contradiction) which is neither actual nor imaginatively possible. This consideration leads him, in other passages, to confine our thought to actual operations as the only proper objects of reference—either operations already performed or to be performed. It is only when references to both classes of operations are allowed that the theory becomes at all plausible. For if completed operations can alone be conceived, it becomes impossible to learn any thing new; whereas, on the other hand, if our references are limited to operations to be performed, the theory involves one form of the futuristic paradox: *we can refer only to our future acts.*[31]

But it must not be assumed that Dewey's loyalty to this bizarre theory does not waver. In some passages he definitely admits that our references, although they include

---

[31] Dewey's general bias towards the future frequently combines with his epistemological theory to make "operations to be performed" the exclusive objects of attention. See Chapter VI.

operations, embrace a larger field. The content of an
idea is, then, not a particular operation, e. g., of tasting,
but the distinct *quale* which is experienceable as a result
of the operation.[32] The meaning, as the theory is now
conceived, consists, not in the reference to the verifying
acts, but in the reference to the *quale*. Thus modified,
the thesis becomes merely this; in order for a concept to
be meaningful, it must (among other things) be possible
to specify the operations by means of which the object
referred to may be detected. The primary object of reference need not be an operation, although operations are
essential to test its existence. Furthermore, since these
operations may be past or future, actual or possible,
it follows that a reference to any complex of qualities
or relations is legitimate if it is possible to specify the
conditions under which these *may* be experienced; and,
specifically, a reference to any past event, as such, is
meaningful if, *at that time,* by means of specific operations (including sensible observation), its characters and
relations would have become manifest.[33]

II. *The Practical Character of Objects:* A different
sort of question about meaning must now be raised. Can
a reference to objects whose characters are not verifiable
by any operations, either past or future, be meaningful?
Can we actually have ideas of, and beliefs about, these
" metempirical " entities? Is this possibility denied when
Dewey states that " things are denoted primarily in their
practical relationships "? The problem is further com-
plicated by the distinction Dewey draws between the
existence of an object and its " meaning," which is defined

[32] See above, note 29.
[33] There is a further ambiguity in the term " operation "; does it
signify " mental " as well as " physical " acts?

as " the future responses which it [the object] requires of us or commits us to." [34] For in his statement that " objects are primarily denoted in their practical relationships, as things of doing, suffering, contact, possession and use," [35] is he offering (a) an explanation of his own way of using either the word " object " or the word " denote "; (b) a piece of introspective psychology; or (c) a metaphysical theorem? In the first case, the question is one of arbitrary definition, and no dispute can arise. In the second case, Dewey is indicating an important fact about the human species—that it reacts to natural objects in a practical and emotional way. If we call that fact psychological, it is not necessarily the worse on that account, but the question at issue still remains: does this provide the only way in which objects can be conceived? Can they not also be thought of as they are, in themselves, in their relations with one another? At times Dewey clearly admits this possibility, and states, indeed, that the realization of it marks preëminently the task of science. Certain characteristics of objects are purely functions of their interactions with one another, of the different relationships existing between them; and, consequently, scientific objects need not be defined with respect to any human use.

Scientific meanings were superadded to esthetic and affectional meanings when objects instead of being defined in terms of their consequences in social interactions and discussion were defined in terms of their consequences with respect to one another.[36]

Many critics take an " instrumental " theory of knowledge to signify that the value of knowing is instrumental to the knower. . . . But " instrumentalism " is a theory not about personal dis-

---

[34] *Essays in Experimental Logic,* p. 309.
[35] *Experience and Nature* (1st ed.), p. 32.
[36] *Ibid.,* p. 189.

position and satisfaction in knowing, but about the proper objects of science, what is " proper " being defined in terms of physics.[37]

But it is just as clear that, at other times, Dewey's theory *is* equivalent to a denial of the possibility of conceiving objects as independent of human needs or purposes. In *The Quest for Certainty* scientific objects are described as quasi-fictions, as abstractions constructed to promote the sensory enjoyments of non-cognitive experience:

When this standardized constant [the physical object], the result of series of operations and expressing an indefinite multitude of possible relations among concrete things, is treated as the reality of nature, an instrument made for a purpose is hypostatized into a substance complete and self-sufficient in isolation.[38]

Dewey, then, is not at all consistent in his conception of the nature of objects. In an earlier period, he held that objects—although their existence is given *for* thought and not constituted *by* it—cannot be characterized except in terms of human purposes, desires and needs.[39] This view, however, faces the task of explaining the whole body of physical knowledge; and Dewey's perception of the inadequacy of a " fictional " account of scientific conceptions

[37] *Ibid.,* p. 151.
[38] *The Quest for Certainty,* p. 239. This passage evidences Dewey's antipathy to admitting that abstractions from immediate experience can be real facts. He is also guilty of an invalid disjunction in his stipulation that objects must be either purposive constructs *or* old-fashioned substances. Physical objects may be genuine constituents of events—neither isolated nor self-sufficient—without being " instruments constructed for a purpose." C. I. Lewis, in his *Mind and the World Order,* New York, Scribner's, 1929, p. 52, extends Dewey's thesis even further, so that every reference to objects is *explicitly* purposeful. For a discussion of this radical doctrine, see George Boas, " Mr. Lewis's Theory of Meaning," *Journal of Philosophy,* XXVIII (1931), 319.
[39] *Essays in Experimental Logic,* p. 308.

compelled him to give a contrasting description of them: *viz.*, that they do point to objective relations which physical objects sustain to one another. But he is unwilling to construe this thesis as assuring the metaphysical superiority of such objects (because they characterize nature throughout), and veers back to the position that they are "instrumental to non-cognitive experience" which alone gives us access to reality. In this final reversal of his thought, "the only complete and unadulterated realism" [40] becomes indistinguishable from phenomenalism.

---

[40] *The Quest for Certainty*, p. 240.

CHAPTER VI

FUTURISM

The term "practical" (and its derivatives) which bulked so large in pragmatist discussions was soon revealed as hopelessly ambiguous. In a narrow sense, the term refers to the bare necessities of life; more loosely, it signifies the sum total of goods which man may cherish. Many intellectualistic critics, relying upon the former interpretation, reviled pragmatism as a "bread-and-butter" philosophy, or—as others put it—a rationalization (in the Freudian sense) of American "big business." Dewey has hastened to deny that this is the correct interpretation of the pragmatist doctrine, insisting that "practical" refers to consequences as such *without any specification or restriction of the characters which these may possess.* Practicalism thus loses its distinctive character and shades off into a mere emphasis upon the future. However, it is in this weakened form sufficiently different from its more extreme manifestations to bear a different name; and the term "futurism" has been suggested for this purpose. Dewey's unmistakable bias towards all things future is clearly evidenced in the following passages:

The preoccupation of experience with things which are coming . . . is obvious to any one whose interest in experience is empirical. Since we live forward; since we live in a world where changes are going on whose issue means our weal or woe; since every act of ours modifies these changes and hence is fraught with promise, or charged with hostile energies—what should experience be but a future implicated in a present! [1]

What is going on in the environment, is the concern of the organ-

[1] *Creative Intelligence*, p. 12.

ism; not what is already " there " in accomplished and finished
form. . . . Experience exhibits things in their unterminated
aspect moving toward determinate conclusions. The finished and
done with is of import as affecting the future, not on its own
account: in short, because it is not, really, done with.[2]

What is done with, what is just " there," is of concern only in
the potentialities which it may indicate. As ended, as wholly
given, it is of no account.[3]

If Dewey means merely that the future is more important, more significant than the past, no reasonable man
would dissent. What is going to be *does* press more
urgently upon our attention than the experiences which
we have already passed through. But from this common-
place, Dewey proceeds to draw psychologically and episte-
mologically important inferences about the nature of ideas
and of meaning; and his reasonings must be examined to
determine, first the precise nature of these inferences,
and, second, whether they follow legitimately from his
premises.

Dewey frequently tends to argue that it is only with
respect to the future that ideas and intelligence are properly definable:

A being which can use given and finished facts as signs of things
to come; which can take given things as evidences of absent
things, can, in that degree, forecast the future; it can form reasonable expectations. It is capable of achieving ideas; it is possessed of intelligence. For use of the given or finished to antici-
pate the consequences of processes going on is precisely what is
meant by " ideas," by " intelligence." [4]

[2] *Ibid.*, p. 13.
[3] *Ibid.*, p. 20.
[4] *Ibid.*, p. 21. But can a temporalist who takes his doctrine seriously
equate the " given " and the " finished " in this fashion? It is this
identification of two fundamentally distinct concepts which is at the root

The problem this passage raises is one of meaning or, more specifically, of reference. In the preceding chapter, we examined Dewey's "practicalistic" answer to this problem, and we shall now investigate the closely related futuristic one. What are the *kinds* of things to which we may meaningfully refer? Must they necessarily be elements of future experience; or, if references to other regions of existence are permissible, must these, in turn, imply future experiences which validate the original act of referring? First, however, the distinction which Dewey draws between cognitive and other references must be noted. Cognitive references occur only in problematic situations; and Dewey, by definition, equates the object of judgment—the referent to which the idea points— with the future experience in which the difficulty will be overcome:

If we refer again to the fact that the genuine antecedent of thought is a situation which is disorganized in its structural elements, we can easily understand how certain contents may be detached and held apart as meanings or references, actual or possible. . . . We can understand how validity of meaning is measured by reference to something . . . which lies beyond it as such—viz., the reconstitution of an experience into which it enters as a method of control.[5]

The thing meaning is one thing; the thing meant is another thing, and is (as already pointed out) a thing presented as not given in the same way as the thing which means. It is something *to be* so given.[6]

And in the more recent terminology of operationalism:

of Dewey's great mistake: his failure to see that the ascertainment of *what is finished* involves the same sort of mental processes as does the prediction of what is to come.

[5] *Essays in Experimental Logic,* pp. 170-1.

[6] *Influence of Darwin on Philosophy,* p. 103 n.

Given data which locate the nature of the problem, there is evoked a thought of an operation which if put into execution may eventuate in a situation in which the trouble or doubt which evoked inquiry will be resolved.[7]

These passages imply that all judgments are predictive, that they explicitly refer to future experience—presumably, of the individual formulating the judgment. But just as Dewey's contention that all judgments are practical foundered upon the rock of judgments of fact, so does his present thesis fall when confronted with the indubitable existence of judgments about the past.[8] As a consequence, Dewey was compelled to modify his futuristic thesis to more modest proportions.

Dewey points out, first, that judgments involving past events arise out of inquiries concerning present or future matters; but the irrelevance of this consideration even he admits. The mere fact that judgments about the past originate in this way does not of itself enable us to decide whether such judgments refer exclusively to the past or not.

But in cognition—Dewey goes on to say—there is no clear-cut distinction between the content of the judgment and the means to its verification. "I have tried to show that *knowledge* where the past is implicated is logically knowledge of past-as-connected-with-present-or-future."[9] The past-present-future is an integral continuum which is the complete object of judgment. If a reference to a past

---

[7] *The Quest for Certainty*, p. 123.

[8] This question was incidentally discussed in a series of papers by Professors Dewey and Lovejoy in the *Journal of Philosophy*. The last of these, in Vol. XXI (1924), 601, gives the references to those which preceded. The present writer's debt to Professor Lovejoy is obvious to any who are familiar with that discussion.

[9] *Journal of Philosophy*, XIX (1922), 309. Dewey's peculiar use of the term "knowledge" will be developed further in Chapter X.

event is cognitive (in the eulogistic sense) it must be accompanied by a reference to future events which are capable of direct presentation in experience. Other references, *e. g.*, pure reminiscences, are labelled " esthetic " meanings, and they have for Dewey apparently no epistemological significance whatever.

The object [of judgment] is some past event in its connection with present and future effects and consequences. The past by itself and *the present by itself* are *both* arbitrary selections which mutilate the complete object of judgment. . . . The past incident is part of the subject matter of inquiry which enters into its object only when referred to a future event or fact. (To avoid further misconception it should be expressly stated that the " future fact " in the last sentence means future to—because a consequence of—a past event, not future to the time of making the judgment; it might be contemporaneous with the latter.) [10]

And in an earlier writing:

Imagine the war done with, and a future historian giving an account of it. The episode is, by assumption, past. But he cannot give a thoughtful account of the war save as he preserves the time sequence; the meaning of each occurrence, as he deals with it, lies in what was future to *it*, though not for the historian. To take it by itself as a complete existence is to take it unreflectively. [11]

These statements illustrate the radical difference between this futurism and the one championed by William James. For James (at times) the meaning of all propositions consisted in future experiences of the one making the judgment, [12] but for Dewey the issue hinges upon the

---

[10] *Ibid.*, XXI (1924), 207-8. The emphasis upon the "complete object of judgment " is clearly a Hegelian survival.

[11] *Democracy and Education*, p. 172.

[12] *Journal of Philosophy, etc.*, I (1904), 674. See also *Pragmatism*, pp. 96-100.

character of the object-referred-to. If it is conceived as isolated, self-enclosed, it cannot be said to be *known;* the event itself has no " meaning," for the meaning of an event is defined as consisting in its consequences.[18] Knowledge, in Dewey's terminology, requires the additional factor of verifiability—sometimes, indeed, the actual verification—of the object of reference in the immediate experience of the would-be knower. In cognition, therefore, the past event referred to must be conceived as connected with a series of consequences reaching to the present and (or) future experience of the person who makes the reference.

It is submitted that a three-fold confusion of considerations is involved in Dewey's argument. First, there is the Hegelian notion that you cannot think of or have knowledge about anything in isolation. In the second place, knowledge is impossible without verification, which means, at the least, that certain implications from the propositions-to-be-known must be capable of direct presentation in experience. But to be so presented, they must (where the original reference is to the past) obviously be future to the events of which they are the consequence. Finally, by calling the verifying data the " meaning " of the events originally referred to, Dewey is then able to say that the meaning of the original judgment about the past is some future (or present) verifying data.

To lay bare the character of this reasoning is a sufficient criticism of it. It is plain that if—as Dewey holds—the

[18] Dewey sometimes uses the term " meaning " to express a property of events as such, and in doing so he wavers between an " organismic " and a " futuristic " conception; sometimes it is the potential consequences, at others it is the total history, which is the meaning of a specific event. In the *Journal of Philosophy,* XXV (1928), 348, Dewey attempts to show that these two views are not incompatible.

" meaning " of an event is its causal or spatio-temporal relation to other events, there is no cogent reason for preferring consequences to causes or conditions as the privileged class of events which confer meaning. If one is going to employ language in this manner, there is no more justification for saying, e. g., that the assassination of Archduke Ferdinand at Sarajevo " meant " the immediate outbreak of the World War than that it " meant " the Bosnian discontent with the oppression of the Dual Monarchy. It is the more frequent verifiability of consequences which makes them for Dewey a privileged class of " meanings," but this supposed advantage is, in truth, illusory, for the certainty which it appears to afford is a specious one. It is an elementary consideration of logic that the assertion of the consequent of an implicative proposition does not allow one to assert the antecedent, and this difficulty cannot be obviated by calling the one the " meaning " of the other. It follows that any knowledge which is not in its primary intent predictive, can never be susceptible of complete verification, for the verification of the implied predictive propositions lends only probability to the original non-predictive assertion.

There is a difficulty inherent in any reference to the past which supplies an additional motive for Dewey's conversion of them into predictive propositions: the basic problem of how a reference to a particular past event is possible at all.

How can the present belief jump out of its present skin, dive into the past, and land upon just the one event (that as past is gone forever) which, by definition, constitutes its truth . . . How [do] we manage to know when one thought lands straight on the devoted head of something past and gone, while another thought comes down on the wrong thing in the past? [14]

[14] *Influence of Darwin on Philosophy*, p. 160.

Dewey's own answer has already been shown to be no answer at all. The mere verification of the consequences of the belief (reference) is not enough. There must be a conceptual location of the event referred to in a schema of temporal relations in which the present reflective act is placed as a component part. Only in so far as the would-be knower is capable of the construction of such a conceptual framework of events, can he meaningfully refer to existents which no longer are or which are not yet.[15] To assign position to a particular past (or future) event involves an implicit reference to that whole system of events which make up the objective order of nature. But this relation to external events serves merely as a means of defining the locus of the event. *At least some* of its characters are inherent in it; while Dewey asserts, though not without waverings and inconsistencies, that consequences alone impart character to an event.

[15] Even then there is no certainty that the reference is correct. Upon the present view, such certainty is impossible of attainment; we must be content with the probability which a proposition acquires from the repeated verification of inferences from it.

CHAPTER VII

CREATIVE INTELLIGENCE AND EMERGENT EVOLUTION

Perhaps the most important postulate in Dewey's entire philosophy is that of the efficacy of intelligence. That man actually " gets things done," that the activity of his intelligence shapes in part the course of natural events is one of the most firmly—not to say fervently—believed of the articles of Dewey's faith. But a further thesis is also defended—that intelligence brings absolute novelties into the world. This was later to develop and has perhaps never commanded the same degree of Dewey's devotion as the first. These, it should be noted, are logically distinct and independent theses, and although Dewey often asserts them together, we shall see that they occasionally conflict in their respective implications.

I. *The Efficacy of Intelligence:* From the time when the importance of biological considerations first impressed itself upon him, Dewey has been tireless in asserting that intelligence is active, effective and useful:

The progress of biology has accustomed our minds to the notion that intelligence is not an outside power presiding supremely but statically over the desires and efforts of man, but is a method of adjustment of capacities and conditions within specific situations.[1]

[The idealistic logic] ignored the temporally intermediate and instrumental place of reflection; and because it ignored and denied this place, it overlooked its essential feature; control of the environment in behalf of human progress and well-being.[2]

If the knower, however defined, is set over against the world to

---

[1] *Influence of Darwin on Philosophy,* p. 68. The Darwinian motivation of this passage is obvious and explicit.

[2] *Essays in Experimental Logic,* p. 22.

be known, knowing consists in possessing a transcript, more or less accurate but otiose, of real things.[3]

Dewey's almost exclusive preoccupation with practical judgments [4] now becomes easily understandable; and his analysis of certain features of those judgments is based directly upon the assumption that intelligence is an operative factor within nature. We recapitulate briefly here those of Dewey's theses, already discussed, which gain support from it:

(a) In Chapter III we saw why Dewey favored the view of a world-in-the-making—that it is only in such a plastic world that intelligence can do its proper work. A radical expression of the conclusion from this is found in the following passage:

The great difference between the conception proposed and that of traditional theory consists in recognition of the objective character of indeterminateness; it is a real property of some natural existences.[5]

(b) Another type of indeterminacy was suggested in Chapter V—the genuineness of the alternatives upon which intelligence must act; this requires no further discussion.[6]

The present assumption has these important epistemological implications for Dewey:

1. He treats the reflective act as a unit; overt bodily and physical activity are assimilated to thinking. By this expedient he hopes to vindicate his thesis that "thought" is efficacious.

[3] *Creative Intelligence,* p. 59.
[4] See Chapter V.
[5] *The Quest for Certainty,* p. 231.
[6] The second characteristic of practical judgments, that they enter actively into the course of events, is a restatement of the major assumption.

[Thinking] involves the explorations by which relevant data are procured and the physical analyses by which they are refined and made precise; it comprises the readings by which information is got hold of, the words which are experimented with, and the calculations by which the significance of entertained conceptions or hypotheses is elaborated. Hands and feet, apparatus and appliances of all kinds are as much a part of it as changes in the brain.[7]

And, in *The Quest for Certainty*, Dewey argues at great length that the act of knowing is such as necessarily to involve a transformation or modification of prior existence:

Knowing is one kind of interaction which goes on within the world. . . . What is known is seen to be a product in which the act of observation plays a necessary rôle. Knowing is seen to be a participant in what is finally known.[8]

But both in the earlier and in the later work, Dewey qualifies—or unsays—this by a significant addition:

This does not mean that some psychic state or act makes the difference in things. . . . It is the physical act which makes the difference, but nevertheless the act is but the complete object of judgment and the judgment is complete as a judgment only in the act.[9]

It is not the "mental" phase of observation which makes the difference.[10]

Dewey's procedure consists, in short, in a redefinition of "thinking" and "knowing" so as to include in their signification the physical acts which are involved in them.[11]

---

[7] *Essays in Experimental Logic*, p. 14.
[8] *The Quest for Certainty*, p. 204.
[9] *Essays in Experimental Logic*, p. 388.
[10] *The Quest for Certainty*, p. 202.
[11] This furnishes a fine example of the fusion of the organismic and practical motivations.

6

But the language of these passages contains an implicit psychophysical dualism which Dewey repudiates. He does not admit that there *are* two types of activity—physical and psychical—no matter how intimate their connection may be conceived to be. In order to avoid this dualism, and the problem of interaction which it raises, Dewey at times is constrained to adopt a radical form of behaviorism.

Thinking is mental, not because of a peculiar stuff which enters into it or of peculiar non-natural activities which constitute it, but because of what physical acts and appliances *do*; the distinctive purpose for which they are employed.[12]

Instrumentalism means a behaviorist theory of thinking and knowing. It means that knowing is literally something which we do; that analysis is ultimately physical and active; and meanings in their logical quality are standpoints, attitudes, and methods of behaving toward facts, and that active experimentation is essential to verification. Put in another way it holds that thinking does not mean any transcendent states or acts suddenly introduced into a previously natural scene, but that the operations of knowing are (or artfully derived from) natural responses of the organism.[13]

A more outspoken and explicit formulation of behaviorism would be hard to find; and if Dewey seriously urged this thesis, it would require further discussion. These pronunciamentos, however, do not mean all that they at first seem to mean; for he is, in other passages, just as explicit in denying that " thinking " is adequately describable in physical terms or that it is reducible to a mathematical function of physical variables. Dewey rejects as inadequate the " description [which] reduces speech to vocalization or making of sounds and thinking to a

---

[12] *Essays in Experimental Logic*, p. 14.   [13] *Ibid.*, pp. 331-2.

silent exercise of the organs of vocalization and other internal structures." [14] He chides the extreme behaviorists who will have nothing to do with awareness, for their own procedure implies " that some behavior, their own, for example, in the observations and analyses whose conclusions they present, is conscious: that is, is aware of what it is about, of what it is doing, and trying to do." [15]

2. Although Dewey can scarcely be placed, therefore, among the ranks of the militant behaviorists of the Watsonian variety, his " behaviorism" is not wholly nugatory. "The main thesis of *Experience and Nature* . . . that human experience is intelligent . . . and emotional behavior," [16] has this important consequence: " representative ideas " which are, for the epistemological dualist, the indispensable condition of all knowing, are ruled out of Dewey's system largely because they are not sufficiently active to comply with the requirements of a creative intelligence:

Knowledge which is merely a reduplication in ideas of what exists already in the world may afford us the satisfaction of a photograph, but that is all. To form ideas whose worth is to be judged by what exists independently of them is not a function that (even if the test could be applied, which seems impossible) goes on within nature or makes any difference there. Ideas that are plans of operations to be performed are integral factors in actions which change the face of the world.[17]

What exactly does this passage mean? Does Dewey wish to assert that representative ideas exist but are super-

[14] J. Ratner, *The Philosophy of John Dewey*, New York, Henry Holt & Co., 1928, p. 102.
[15] *Ibid.*, p. 104.
[16] *Journal of Philosophy*, XXIV (1927), 62.
[17] *The Quest for Certainty*, pp. 137-8. See the next chapter for an argument of Dewey's against epistemological dualism which is based upon the principle of continuity.

numerary and, therefore, negligible, or that they actually have no existence? Both of these contentions are, I think, unsound, although the former does gain some apparent support from the doctrine of the efficacy of intelligence. Dewey is misled because of a simple fallacy; one cannot argue from the efficacy of reflective activity to the dynamic character of *every* component of the process. Paradoxical as it may at first appear, the functional requirement of many ideas is that they be non-functional. For what does intelligent activity imply? It surely includes: (a) a representation of the future state of affairs which will *result* if a certain act should be performed; (b) a representation of past experiences from the uniformities in which the future effect of the contemplated act can be inferred; and therefore (c) a judgment as to some general law of cause and effect. But at least the past experiences and the general laws can be known only through " ideas *about* what exists independently of them." And the " worth " of these ideas obviously depends upon the correctness of their representation of these independent facts. Therefore, it is only by his failure to analyze the situation sufficiently—or, rather, by his refusal to recognize the products of analysis as realities—that Dewey makes a show of ruling out representative ideas from his world-picture.

Dewey's metaphysical views also bear the deep impress of his belief in the efficacy of intelligence. After he gave up—largely because of it—his allegiance to monistic Idealism, it was his faith in this principle which prevented him from embracing mechanistic evolutionism or other absolutistic theories. When he turned, in *Experience and Nature,* to the task of formulating a metaphysics, he found in a type of emergent evolutionism the conception most congenial to this fundamental conviction.[18]

[18] This is discussed more fully below, pp. 74-81.

II. *Intelligence as Creative of Novelty:* Dewey's second thesis about the activity of intelligence—its creative novelty—has also important consequences in his philosophy. He now expressly denies that intelligence is to be understood after the strict Darwinian formula. It does not exist solely for the service of animal needs, or of propensities already evolved; for it can and does bring in new ends of its own.

As a matter of fact, the pragmatic theory of intelligence means that the function of mind is to project new and more complex ends—to free experience from routine and from caprice. Not the use of thought to accomplish purposes already given either in the mechanism of the body or in that of the existent state of society, but the use of intelligence to liberate and liberalize action is the pragmatic lesson.[19]

Thus intelligence is *not* merely an " instrument of adjustment or adaptation to a particular environing situation," [20] for " a pragmatic intelligence is a creative intelligence, not a routine mechanic." [21]

" To catch mind in its connexion with the entrance of the novel into the course of the world is to be on the road to see that intelligence is itself the most promising of all novelties." [22] This passage takes Dewey beyond a merely functional novelty. Intelligence involves both " imaginative forecast of the future " and " imaginative recovery of the bygone." [23] " What is unique . . . is the property of awareness or perception. Because of this property, the initial stage is capable of being judged in the light of its

[19] *Creative Intelligence,* p. 63.
[20] *Essays in Experimental Logic,* p. 93.
[21] *Creative Intelligence,* p. 64.
[22] *Ibid.,* p. 66.
[23] *Ibid.,* p. 14. Dewey, for reasons noted in the preceding chapter, emphasizes the former and almost completely disregards the latter.

probable course and consequence. There is anticipation. Each successive event being a stage in a serial process is both expectant and commemorative." [24] Since he denies that this phenomenon points to any " separate kind of existence called psychic or mental," it becomes questionable what type of novelty he wishes to establish for awareness. In *Experience and Nature* this is treated as one example of the general problem of emergence, and his discussion of that topic will now be examined.

Dewey posits a serial order of natural events, which falls into definite, well-marked stages.[25] At one stage in the history of our universe, no living or conscious beings existed. Upon the occurrence of certain groupings of inanimate objects, life appeared. Mind developed only later, after living creatures had acquired a certain degree of organization. Each of these stages is a genuine addition to the cosmic scene, *i. e.,* its existence is not logically implicit in the state of affairs from which it developed. This all sounds like a familiar form of the theory of emergent evolution, but since Dewey apparently wishes to deny some of the characteristic implications of that theory, his reasonings on this point must be scrutinized carefully. Life, we are told, marks the appearance of " need-demand-satisfaction " in a world to which that factor had hitherto been foreign. But a word of caution must be added; these terms are not to be interpreted in a subjectivistic or psychological sense:

By need is meant a condition of tensional distribution of energies such that the body is in a condition of uneasy or unstable equilibrium. By demand or effort is meant the fact that this state is manifested in movements which modify environing bodies in

[24] *Experience and Nature,* p. 101.
[25] I summarize here an argument contained for the most part in Chapter VII of *Experience and Nature.*

ways which react upon the body, so that its characteristic pattern of active equilibrium is restored. By satisfaction is meant this recovery of equilibrium pattern, consequent upon the changes of environment due to interactions with the active demands of the organism.[26]

Since physical events at the inorganic level are not characterized by this type of activity, life—it must be repeated—introduces a new mode of interaction of events into the natural order. The difference between the animate and the inanimate "lies in the way in which physico-chemical energies are interconnected and operate . . . respectively." [27] To such organic activity, Dewey gives the name "psychophysical " [28]; this is so coördinated that the parts nourish the whole, and the whole interpenetrates the parts.

Pervasive operative presence of the whole in the part and of the part in the whole constitutes susceptibility—the capacity of feeling—whether or no this potentiality be actualized in plant life. . . . With organization, bias becomes interest, and satisfaction a good or value and not a mere satiation of wants or repletion of deficiencies.[29]

Furthermore, when animals become complex and develop distance receptors, they virtually react to the future. Their actions become differentiated into the preparatory and the consummatory; then, when " the immediate preparatory response is suffused with the consummatory tone of sex or food or security to which it contributes . . . sensitivity,

[26] *Experience and Nature,* p. 253.

[27] *Ibid.,* p. 254.

[28] This use of the term " psychophysical " is peculiar to Dewey and should not be confused with the more common meanings.

[29] *Ibid.,* p. 256. It would at first appear that Dewey introduces rather surreptitiously what are usually regarded as conscious phenomena. It is not clear, however, that " interest," " value," etc., are used in a psychological sense, and what follows tends to negate that possibility.

the capacity, is actualized as feeling." [30] Feelings become differentiated in direct proportion with the number and variety of responses:

Complex and active animals *have*, therefore, feelings which vary abundantly in quality, corresponding to distinctive directions and phases . . . of activities, bound up in distinctive connections with environmental affairs. They have them, but they do not know they have them. [31]

Dewey further contends that "mental" phenomena (in his sense of the term) do not appear before language. Then

qualities of feeling become significant of objective differences in external things and of episodes past and to come. This state of things in which qualitatively different feelings are not just had but are significant of objective differences, is mind. [32]

Without language, the qualities of organic action that are feelings are pains, pleasures, odors, colors, noises, tones, only potentially and proleptically. With language they are discriminated and identified. They are then "objectified"; they are immediate traits of things. This "objectification" is not a miraculous ejection from the organism or soul into external things, nor an illusory attribution of psychical entities to physical things. The qualities never were "in" the organism; they always were qualities of interactions in which both extra-organic things and organisms partake. . . . They are as much qualities of the things engaged as of the organism. [33]

[30] *Ibid.*, p. 257.

[31] *Ibid.*, p. 258. "Knowing" is evidently used in this passage in the ordinary sense of awareness, uncolored by Dewey's epistemology. Since he distinguishes between "feelings" and awareness of them, it becomes all the more evident that he intended to employ the terms "interest" and "value" in a biological or quasi-biological sense.

[32] *Ibid.*, p. 258.

[33] *Ibid.*, pp. 258, 259. "Quality" is evidently equivalent to sense-datum, except that Dewey does not like the latter term since it involves, he thinks, a mistaken epistemology.

Dewey, it thus appears, asserts unmistakably that sense qualities have no existence except as the result of a particular interaction of an organism and a suitable environment. They are, then, genuine emergents, for they are additions to nature of a kind of entity which was previously nowhere to be found. He also seems to recognize another type of emergent which enters the natural scene at this time; namely, meanings.[34] Dewey redefines "mind" as the field of operative meanings. These also do not exist without language, since Dewey refuses to call "meaningful" the signalling acts of the higher animals. He connects the occurrence of meanings with language, because he thinks that he can, in this way, escape the pitfall of psychophysical dualism, and so keep his theory "naturalistic." But is this expedient sufficient for his purpose? Can he fit into one coherent scheme physical events, immediate qualities, and meanings? The dualistic

[34] Dewey employs the term "meaning" in at least three distinguishable senses. (1) He attempts at times to describe meaning as a relationship between purely physical events. Events because of causal connection (or otherwise) present a definite spatio-temporal coexistence or succession. This relationship is purely mathematical or physical. To say, then, that "smoke means fire" is equivalent to the statement that two physical events are causally related to one another. (2) Dewey at other times gives a "behavioristic" interpretation of meaning. Meaning is a property of a distinctive type of behavior, and specifically—in *Experience and Nature*, Chapter V—of social behavior. Meaning is a method of action, a way of using things. He attempts to describe this situation without bringing in awareness, although he does not always succeed. (3) Finally, Dewey has a frankly dualistic conception of meaning. Meaning is the *apprehension* of the relation of events to one another. In order for this to take place, there must be presented, at a single moment of experience, not only the compresent data, but also the things pointed to or meant, which are *not* literally present. In Dewey's own terminology, the thing meant must be "vicariously present" or "present-as-absent." This is a highly anomalous mode of occurrence, and significantly different from the existence of an ordinary quality. In this discussion, unless otherwise noted, the third sense of meaning will be understood.

solution which denies this possibility is extremely distasteful to Dewey because of its breach of continuity.[35] To him " philosophical dualism is but a formulated recognition of an impasse in life," [36] and, for it, he substitutes the notion of historical development. There are three levels or plateaus on which events interact, and each of these has its own distinctive properties. In what sense, then, does Dewey preserve a continuity between these levels? Although his reasonings upon this point are extremely elusive, he appears to waver between two views as to the relation of physical events, immediate qualities and meanings to one another.

(1) The problem is made to vanish by means of a suitable set of definitions. All existences are bare occurrences, events. The term " natural event " is not restrictive. Any actual occurrence is *ipso facto* a natural event. Furthermore, those things which are ordinarily taken to be existences are actually adjectives of existence: " ' Matter,' or the physical, is a character of events when they occur at a certain level of interaction. It is not itself an event or existence." [37] The data of perception are universals, not particulars: " *What* is perceived are meanings, rather than just events or existences." [38] " When it is denied that we are conscious of *events* as such it is not meant that we are not aware of *objects*. . . . Objects are events *with* meanings." [39] If all existences are particular events, and the qualities and meanings which characterize

---

[35] See next chapter.
[36] *Experience and Nature*, p. 241.
[37] *Ibid.*, p. 262.
[38] *Ibid.*, p. 317.
[39] *Ibid.*, p. 318. In passages such as these, Dewey seems to flirt with contemporary Platonism as manifested in logical realism and the " essence " theory of Critical Realism and Objective Relativism.

them merely universals, there would be no problem of relating different realms of existences, but in its stead we should have the equally serious task of linking, in some intelligible sense, existences which just *are* with the characters—qualities and meanings—which are supposed to apply in some fashion to them, while retaining their universality and non-existential status.[40]

(2) Dewey does not attempt to solve this problem— no doubt because he states elsewhere that qualities and meanings do exist and, as such, are necessarily particulars. "To say that [qualities] are *felt,* is to say that they come to independent and intrinsic existence on their own account." [41] " Immediate qualities, being extruded from the object of science, were left thereby hanging loose from the ' real' object. Since their *existence* could not be denied, they were gathered together into a psychic realm of being." [42] " Meanings existentially occurring are ideas." [43] But now a new problem faces Dewey, for if specific instances of qualities are existents, *where* do they exist? And similarly with meanings. Can they, like physical objects, be localized? In another discussion,[44] Dewey goes so far as to say that *no* object can be assigned a specific spatio-temporal locus; the concept of locus must be operationally defined, and a thing is thus " located "

---

[40] A bifurcation of " adjectives " would still remain.

[41] *Experience and Nature,* p. 267.

[42] *Ibid.,* p. 264.

[43] *Ibid.,* p. 305. " Idea " corresponds to the third type of meaning distinguished in note 15, *supra.* Dewey wavers constantly between the first and third senses of this term. In the first sense, " meaning " signifies the objective relation between events, and an apprehension of this relation is also needed; this Dewey calls " idea." When used in the third sense, " meaning " is the particular apprehension, and thus an additional apprehension or awareness would be supernumerary.

[44] *Ibid.,* pp. 195-7.

wherever it has important effects.[45] This comes perilously close to rendering the very notion of existence meaningless, for the categories of space and time and definite position in a space-time system usually enter into the definition of an existent. Dewey recognizes that there is a problem in localizing mind, but he thinks he can avoid it because in his system mind is a function which involves a temporal spread of events. Although this expedient obviates the necessity of a substance-view of mind, it does not help us to determine what type of event an individual meaning or idea is. Dewey offers this statement in explanation:

[When we think of absent objects, such as a friend or an enemy] there is something present in organic action which acts as a surrogate for the remote things signified. . . . This something now present is not just the activity of the laryngeal and vocal apparatus. . . . The ideas are qualities of events in all the parts of organic structure which have ever been implicated in actual situations of concern with extra-organic friends and enemies:— presumably in proprioreceptors and organ-receptors with all their connected glandular and muscular mechanisms.[46]

This passage is equivocal, for it may mean either of two things: (a) the idea (the meaning as an existent) is the recurrence—without the presence of the external stimulus —of the same bodily set which the organism possessed when reacting directly to the stimulus. This is the behavioristic account of meaning, but this " meaning " is in no sense equivalent to the vicarious presence which Dewey elsewhere insists upon as an essential component of the " idea." (b) The bodily set is a necessary and sufficient

[45] This notion Dewey no doubt derived from Whitehead's denial of " simple location." See A. N. Whitehead, *Science and the Modern World*, p. 133 and *passim*.
[46] *Op. cit.*, p. 292.

condition for the existence of the idea, but is not the idea. The status of the idea still remains unexplained.[47] Dewey sometimes says that it is a neutral entity, a subsistent, but this explanation is certainly subordinate in his mind, and, in any case, involves the difficulties inherent in logical realism. Because of this equivocation and his consequent failure to recognize whole-heartedly the implications of his theory of emergence, Dewey's philosophy of nature remains, in its essential features, blurred and confusing. When he admits the empirical phenomena upon which the hypothesis of psychophysical dualism is based, he has no adequate or coherent account of these facts to offer as an alternative. But he also, at times, denies the existence of some of these ("mental") phenomena, and the logical situation then becomes completely altered. In the next chapter we shall see additional reasons why Dewey's position on these issues has been so vacillating, for the principle of continuity has implications which are incompatible with the belief in any genuine emergence.

[47] Mr. Morris attempts an elucidation of this in his *Six Theories of Mind*, p. 299: "Dewey's position must be that surrogate objects, often called images, are component aspects of the behaving organism when the response is implicit, nascent, and tentative. This does not mean that the image simply is a movement, but rather that the object called the 'organism' is a system of events which includes under certain conditions those events which appear when one thinks of friend or enemy." This passage is itself by no means clear, but if I understand him, Mr. Morris is committed to a conception of the "organism" which is, to say the least, awkward—one which the biologist would have great difficulty in recognizing. For it would seem that the "organism" contains, as a component "aspect" of itself (*i. e.*, as a part of itself in the same sense as any group contains one of its members as a part of it) any imaginal characters which may appear to it. This way of defining "organism," although useful for the purposes of objective relativism, will hardly be serviceable to the scientist.

CHAPTER VIII

CONTINUITY

In the preceding chapter an examination was made of the workings of the conception of emergence in Dewey's thought, and through it attention was directed toward those aspects of nature which appear to exhibit irresoluble discontinuities—to conflict with the traditional maxim *natura non facit saltus*. We turn now to a side of his philosophy which illustrates a contrary tendency—a tendency to treat the principle of rigorous continuity as axiomatic. It will become evident that a presumption of continuity has served as one of the most effective weapons in Dewey's philosophic armory, for it has been directed against such diverse doctrines as psychophysical dualism, " spectator " theories of knowledge, neo-realism and one form of ethical idealism. Since he has never—at least, to the present writer's knowledge—given a definition of what he means by continuity, it is best not to attempt to formulate one at this point. Instead, several illustrations of his reliance upon it will be presented to serve as the basis for a subsequent definition.

(1) Dewey rejects psychophysical dualism because it implies a breach of continuity in nature:

Neither the plain man nor the scientific inquirer is aware, as he engages in his reflective activity, of transition from one sphere of existence to another. He knows no two fixed worlds— reality on one side and mere subjective ideas on the other; he is aware of no gulf to cross. . . . The fundamental assumption is *continuity*.[1]

The occurrence of hallucinations and dreams has some-

[1] *Essays in Experimental Logic*, p. 87.

times been advanced as an argument for psychophysical dualism. Dewey replies:

The logical assumption is that consciousness is outside of the real object . . . and has the power . . . of infecting real things with subjectivity. . . . This assumption makes consciousness supernatural in the literal sense of the word . . . and . . . the conception can be accepted by one who accepts the doctrine of biological continuity only after every other way of dealing with the facts has been exhausted.[2]

(2) Neo-realism, which is, in its " pan-objectivism," directly opposed to psychophysical dualism, violates the principle of continuity in a different fashion:

Much may be said about that other great rupture of continuity which analytic realism would maintain: that between the world and the knower as something outside of it, engaged in an otiose contemplative survey of it. . . . Changed social conditions not only permit but demand that intelligence be placed within the procession of events.[3]

(3) A similar argument is advanced against all " spectator " theories of knowledge:

Traditional theories of mind and its organ of knowledge isolate them from continuity with the natural world. They are in a literal sense of the word, super-natural or extra-natural.[4]

There is no separate " mind " gifted in and of itself with a faculty of thought; such a conception of thought ends in postulating the mystery of a power outside of nature and yet able to intervene within it.[5]

---

[2] *Creative Intelligence*, p. 35.
[3] *Essays in Experimental Logic*, pp. 72-3.
[4] *The Quest for Certainty*, p. 230.
[5] *Ibid.*, p. 227. This provides another example of Dewey's inability to make any sense of psychophysical dualism. That doctrine implies for him two completely unrelated worlds which have no intelligible connection with one another.

These passages indicate that Dewey tends to use " continuity " so vaguely, and to press his assumption of it so far, that he tends to dispose on purely *a priori* grounds of questions concerning the actual amount of empirical differentness there is between things. Whether " minds gifted . . . with a faculty of thought " exist, or whether awareness occurs and is not describable in physical terms —these are questions of fact; you cannot settle them, as Dewey seems disposed to do, by merely saying that if they *did* exist, there would be more discontinuity in nature than you like. Obviously there *is* some discontinuity *in some sense;* that Dewey recognizes this will become apparent in what immediately follows.[6]

(4) Dewey rejects both mechanistic and spiritualistic metaphysics because their conceptions of causality split in two what is essentially a single continuous historical process. Thus, although both describe certain important characters of the natural world,

The notion of causal explanation involved in both conceptions implies a breach in the continuity of historic process; the gulf created has then to be bridged by an emission or transfer of force.[7]

The real existence is the history in its entirety, the history as just what it is. The operations of splitting it up into two parts and then having to unite them again by appeal to causative power are equally arbitrary and gratuitous.[8]

---

[6] It is not true, as Dewey supposes, that spectator theories imply that knowledge is not conditioned by natural factors; nor do they assert that the knower is outside of the world to be cognized. They do assume that there exist some *cognoscenda* (things-to-be-known) whose characters are not modified by the cognitive processes by which they are known.

[7] *Experience and Nature*, p. 273; see also pp. 99-100.

[8] *Ibid.*, p. 275.

Once admit, says Dewey, that existence is temporal, historic, and we need not assign different parts of the history to different realms of being. However, scarcely consistent with his more extreme expressions of continuity is his admission that there are several levels of existence,[9] and that "each one of these levels having its own characteristic empirical traits has its own categories."[10] For not only do new modes of activity enter the natural scene at certain stages of the total history, but the emergence of new modes of existence also furnishes clear evidence of a fundamental cleavage within nature. An intense, if vague, devotion to the principle of continuity prevents Dewey from accepting the dualisms to which his reasoning seems to lead; yet he does not offer any satisfactory alternative to them, nor does he, in fact, consistently escape them.

(5) In Dewey's appeal to continuity in the field of values we may discern a use of the term which is at the same time more modest and more in conformity with the facts. The realm of ideals is not cut off from the world of every-day experience, but grows out of it and represents the possibilities of its development. Any philosophy which lends support

to the practical and current divorce of the "ideal" from the natural world makes it a thing to be dreaded for other than professional reasons. . . . Such a cut-off, ideal world is impotent for direction and control and change of the natural world. . . . If philosophers could aid in making it clear to a troubled humanity that ideals are continuous with natural events, that they but represent their possibilities, and that recognized possibilities form methods for a conduct which may realize them in

[9] Distinguished in preceding chapter.
[10] *Op. cit.,* p. 272.

7

fact, philosophers would enforce the sense of a social calling and responsibility.[11]

In a more recent statement of his *credo* Dewey tells us that his " faith " " implies that the course and material of experience give support and stay to life, and *that its possibilities provide all the ends and ideals that are to regulate conduct.*" [12] These are admirable expressions of a this-worldly moral philosophy; and, although the objection that no effective historical ideal is ever wholly realizable may be literally true, it is irrelevant; for, while we may always imagine things more perfect than they can actually *be,* it is still the case that, except as ideals are employed to aid us in approximating them in fact, they are, as Dewey contends, mere luxuries which deaden significant activity.

" Continuity," as employed in this last argument, is so broad in meaning that it is likely to be denied by nobody; for to assert that two events are parts of a continuous process signifies no more than that they are related to, and interact with, one another. Thus continuity in no sense is equivalent to qualitative identity. It excludes dualism (or pluralism) only if those doctrines are incompatible with the notion of interaction, which they are not. In this innocuous sense continuity and emergence do not at all conflict. Professor Bode has offered this as the proper interpretation of Dewey's use of the principle: " A novel trait is continuous with the antecedent situation from which it emerges, in the sense that it occurs as the result

[11] *Essays in Experimental Logic,* p. 72. These remarks were directed against the thesis of the " new realism " which placed ideals in a realm of subsistent entities. For a similar argument against objective idealism, see *supra,* Chapter III.

[12] " What I Believe," *Forum,* 83 (1930), 176. " Experience " has its extended meaning in this passage.

of an orderly process of change taking place in this situation." [13] And in one late passage Dewey explicitly identifies the continuous with the relational: " The occurrence of problematic and unsettled situations is due to the *characteristic union of the discrete or individual and the continuous or relational.*" [14] Bode, therefore, discards representationism *only in so far as it denies interaction between idea and object.*

The objects concerned necessarily remain wholly indifferent. . . . The accusation of " supernaturalism " does not have reference to the advent of novelty as such, but to the belief in a novelty that is so " external to the system dealt with by the physical sciences " that all the king's horses and all the king's men are unable to put the *disjecta membra* together again.[15]

Therefore, the dualist who holds that ideas have a natural origin—that is, do not exist except as a result of the interaction of a definite set of physical and physiological factors—and that these ideas, when they exist, can serve as links in a chain of causation, cannot be charged with a breach of continuity, in this sense, merely because he also holds that they are not describable in the same terms as physical objects.

It is only when continuity is understood to imply qualitative identity that Dewey's strictures against these theories becomes even pertinent. But the belief that such continuity holds throughout nature is a pure assumption, and it is one of the most perilous of all assumptions for both science and philosophy; for it tends to hasty and dogmatic unifications and to a blindness to the actual

[13] B. F. Bode, " Intelligence and Behavior," *Journal of Philosophy,* XVIII (1921), 14.

[14] *The Quest for Certainty,* p. 234.

[15] *Loc. cit.,* p. 14. But the epistemological dualist who is also a psycho-physical dualist need not deny interaction.

diversity of things. It is important to observe that Dewey works his " continuity " in both directions. Sometimes he starts with qualities or processes found in " lower-level " phenomena, in inanimate objects or in living but unconscious, or non-reflective, organisms; at other times, he starts from the other end, and reads back into pre-human nature those characters of human experience which were formerly regarded as distinctively mental. Professor Woodbridge describes Dewey's thesis in these terms:

If we are unstable, there is instability in it [nature]; if we are contradictory, there is contradiction in it; if we are hopeful, there is possibility—one might dare to say, hope—in it; if we err, there is something like error in it; if we are incomplete, there is incompleteness in it. And all this *does not mean that we are the exclusive instances of all such traits of nature. We are samples of them.*[16]

This interpretation is based in part upon the following passage:

A naturalistic metaphysics is bound to consider reflection as itself a natural event occurring *within* nature because of traits of the latter . . . Traits of reflection are as truly indicative or evidential of the traits of *other* things as are the traits of these events . . . The world must actually be such as to generate ignorance and inquiry; doubt and hypothesis; trial and temporal conclusions.[17]

The complete passage (which is too long to quote in full) seems to waver bafflingly between the two views which have been noted, Does Dewey mean merely that the characteristics of human thinking (uncertainty, ambiguity, alternatives, etc.,) are as real facts as those assured and fixed characters assigned to physical objects, or does

[16] F. J. E. Woodbridge, " Experience and Dialectic," *Journal of Philosophy*, XXVII (1930), 269. Italics mine.
[17] *Experience and Nature*, pp. 68, 69.

he wish to assert that all of the characters of human thought must be ascribed to pre-human events as well? Even though the former may be the view more frequently expressed by him, it is true that he has also definitely supported the latter:

To me human affairs, associative and personal, are projections, continuations, complications, of the nature which exists in the physical and pre-human world. . . . For this reason, there are in nature both foregrounds and backgrounds, heres and theres, centers and perspectives, foci and margins. If there were not, the story and scene of man would involve a complete break with nature, the insertion of unaccountable and unnatural conditions and factors. . . . One who believes in continuity may argue that, since human experience exhibits such traits as Santayana denies to nature, the latter *must* contain their prototypes.[18]

Although Dewey is quite right in insisting that no metaphysical theory can render the occurrence of any actual event or process a contradiction, it is a very different thing to assert the fundamental homogeneity of nature. Certainly we should like to see, in a more detailed fashion than Dewey provides us, how, for example, an act of reflective thought is a " projection, continuation or complication " of astronomical phenomena, or in what sense the movements of the electron within the atom are a prototype of the poetic imaginings of a creative artist.[19] This identity type of continuity obviously excludes the possibility of any genuine emergence (for which Dewey argued so effectively in the preceding chapter), since its

[18] *Journal of Philosophy*, XXIV (1927), 58; a reply to Santayana's review of *Experience and Nature* which appeared in the same journal, XXII (1925), 680.

[19] This criticism, it is granted, has point only within the framework of physical realism; but Dewey seems to accept that doctrine in *Experience and Nature* (2nd ed.), pp. 3a-1.

" categorical imperative " is to make identifications, postulating them when they are not to be found in what is
observed. The fountain-head of this reasoning is the
pseudo-axiom *e nihilo nihil fit,* and the only causal
processes which it recognizes are those in which one can
read back into the cause all of the characters and entities
which are manifested in the effect. But this dogma is so
incongruous with Dewey's more usual assertion of emergence that one can only marvel that he should have ever
attempted to incorporate both into his philosophy.[20]

---

[20] The incompatibility of these two principles is discussed fully in the
concluding chapter of this essay.

CHAPTER IX

MORALISM

Dewey is not among the philosophers who are primarily interested in man in his cognitive capacity. Although the major portion of this essay has been devoted to his views on epistemology and metaphysics, he has throughout his career been deeply concerned with the problems of ethics. One would, therefore, naturally seek to ascertain his answers to such questions as these: What is the nature of the moral judgment? Does it differ in type or in subject matter from other judgments? Is there a peculiar moral faculty? What bearing, if any, does man's concern with values have upon metaphysics? The scope of the present work, however, prevents a detailed discussion of all of these topics; and for our purpose it must suffice to illustrate the profound and far-reaching influence of moral considerations upon Dewey's conception of knowledge and of the function of philosophy.

Dewey's fundamental principle, that man is at bottom a valuing creature, that he is "constructed to think in terms of welfare," may be termed "moralism" if the signification of that expression is enlarged to include attitudes appropriate to all value situations. "Success and failure," Dewey once said, "are the primary ' categories ' of life." [1] It is this conviction—coupled with his craving for "continuity"—which has furnished Dewey one of his major problems: the unification of scientific and ethical thinking.

I became more and more troubled by the intellectual scandal that seemed to be involved in the current (and traditional) dualism in logical standpoint between something called "science"

---

[1] *Creative Intelligence*, p. 13.

on the one hand and something called "morals" on the other. I have long felt that the construction of a logic . . . which would apply without abrupt breach of continuity to the fields designated by both of the words, is at once our needed theoretical solvent and the supply of our greatest practical want.[2]

One of the most genuine problems of modern life is the reconciliation of the scientific view of the universe with the claims of the moral life.[3]

The greatest dualism which now weighs humanity down, [is] the split between the material, the mechanical, the scientific and the moral and the ideal.[4]

How is this breach between moral and scientific judgments to be healed? Judgments of value, it must be remembered, constitute in Dewey's theory a species of judgments of practice. They do not exist apart from activity,[5] nor is " the determination of the right or wrong course of action . . . dependent upon an independent determination of some ghostly things called value-objects —whether their ghostly character is attributed to their existing in some transcendental eternal realm or in some realm called states of mind." [6] Both the belief in a peculiar moral faculty, and the assumption that the subject matter of morals is sharply cut off from the field of the sciences, are thus branded as definitely false. To recover

[2] *Contemporary American Philosophy,* p. 23. Cf. also *The Quest for Certainty,* p. 18.
[3] *Essays in Honor of William James,* p. 63.
[4] *Reconstruction in Philosophy,* New York, Holt, 1920, p. 173.
[5] *Essays in Experimental Logic,* p. 358.
[6] *Ibid.,* p. 358. Since, for Dewey, value judgments are a class of practical judgments, the present discussion of his attempt to assimilate factual judgments to value judgments may appear to be a mere repetition of the argument developed in Chapter V. This is in part true, but a separate treatment is justified because of the slightly different twist in the reasoning, and because of the vital implications which it contains for philosophy.

for morals its rightful place in the scheme of things, philosophy must show how science is nothing but an outgrowth of man's moral endeavor.

Dewey thinks the way to this truth is shown clearly by his genetic account of the cognitive experience. Without repeating prior analyses, attention may be called to the following passages to illustrate his persistent assertion that man's whole existence centers about values, and that thinking arises only when and where values are at stake:

Our constant and inalienable concern is with good and bad, prosperity and failure, and hence with choice. We are constructed to think in terms of value, of bearing upon welfare.[7]

In a vital, though not the conventional, sense all men think with a moral bias and concern, the "immoral" man as truly as the righteous man.[8]

Reflection also implies concern with the issue—a certain sympathetic identification of our own destiny, if only dramatic, with the outcome of the course of events. . . . The flagrant partisanship of human nature is evidence of the intensity of the tendency to identify ourselves with one possible course of events, and to reject the other as foreign. . . . We desire this or that outcome. *One wholly indifferent to the outcome does not follow or think about what is happening at all.*[9]

These quotations express an important truth. Human thought is motivated by desire, and the matters dealt with by reflection are usually significant and important: the "solution" of a problem has at least imagined, if not real, value. But these observations refer legitimately to the *context* of thinking; they have, in strictness, no bearing upon the character of our thought-content. When Dewey

[7] *Experience and Nature* (1st ed.), p. 32.
[8] *Ibid.*, p. 33.
[9] *Democracy and Education*, p. 172. Italics mine.

forgets this simple consideration, he is led to make statements about the nature of knowledge and philosophy
which are no less than astonishing.

What we know, Dewey would now have us believe, is
inevitably conditioned by our needs and desires. Philosophy, in particular, is nothing but an outgrowth of social
conditions, and, the content of a system of philosophy
must be, therefore, a reflection of the emotional and
affective reaction of the thinker to his environment. He
hails as the great achievement of pragmatism its recognition of this true conception of the origin, purpose and
function of philosophy.

Philosophy originated not out of intellectual material, but out
of social and emotional material.[10]

Instead of impersonal and purely speculative endeavors to con-
template as remote beholders the nature of absolute things-in-
themselves, *we have a living picture of the choice of thoughtful
men about what they would have life to be,* and to what ends
they would have men shape their intelligent activities.[11]

Even more emphatic is the passage which now follows:

The intellectual registrations which constitute a philosophy are
generative just because they are selective and eliminative exag-
gerations. While purporting to say that such and such is and
always *has* been the purport of the record of nature, in effect
they proclaim that such and such *should* be the significant value
to which mankind should loyally attach itself. . . . Discuss
[philosophic ideas] as revelations of eternal truth and something
almost childlike or something beyond possibility of decision
enters in; discuss them as selections from existing culture by

---

[10] *Reconstruction in Philosophy,* p. 25.
[11] *Ibid.,* p. 26 (my italics). We have not strayed from the main discussion (Dewey's contention that knowledge is conditioned by needs and
desires), because the " sociological " interpretation of philosophy is but
an outstanding implication of this thesis.

means of which to articulate forces which the author believed should and would dominate the future, and they become preciously significant aspects of human history.[12]

Philosophy will not "find itself" until it awakes to a full consciousness of its true nature:

The moment the complicity of the personal factor in our philosophic valuations . . . is recognized fully, frankly, and generally, that moment a new era in philosophy will begin.[13]

This fact [that all men think with a moral bias and concern] seems to me of great importance for philosophy; it indicates that in some sense all philosophy is a branch of morals.[14]

Dewey concludes from all this that " the task of future philosophy is to clarify men's ideas as to the social and moral strifes of their own day. Its aim is to become so far as is humanly possible an organ for dealing with these conflicts." [15] Let the philosopher abandon, once for all, his futile attempts at metaphysical construction for the more fruitful activity which promotes right conduct and the enhancement of empirical values. In Dewey's final words on the subject:

A philosophy which abandoned its guardianship of fixed realities, values and ideals would find a new career for itself. The meaning of science in terms of science, in terms of knowledge of the actual, may well be left to science itself. Its meaning in terms of the great human uses to which it may be put, its meaning in the service of possibilities of secure value, offers a field for exploration which cries out from very emptiness.[16]

After such sweeping statements, it is instructive to

[12] *Philosophy and Civilization*, New York, Minton, Balch, 1931, p. 8.
[13] *Essays in Experimental Logic*, p. 327.
[14] *Experience and Nature* (1st ed.), p. 33.
[15] *Reconstruction in Philosophy*, p. 26.
[16] *The Quest for Certainty*, p. 311.

show how—in other passages—Dewey refutes himself on each of these points; how he contends that inquiry demands a certain impartiality which is indispensable for its success, that knowledge is more than a statement of desiderata, and that metaphysics is both a possible and a highly valuable subject of study. In some of his later writings Dewey admits, and even insists, that curiosity, the love of problems for their own sake, develops at a certain stage of biological evolution; and that this disinterestedness is distinctive of scientific activity. He is, at such times, quite willing to grant that the scientist (or any reflective inquirer) may consider problems which have no value components whatever except, perhaps, the aesthetic enjoyment derived either from the intellectual effort itself or from the anticipated satisfaction of intellectual curiosity.

A disciplined mind takes delight in the problematic, and cherishes it until a way out is found that approves itself upon examination. . . . The scientific attitude may almost be defined as that which is capable of enjoying the doubtful. . . . No one gets far intellectually who does not have an interest in problems as such.[17]

Dewey could scarcely have believed that all thought is marked by a " moral bias and concern " or that there is an inevitable " complicity of the personal factor in our philosophic valuations " when he said this: " To accomplish its tasks [thought] must achieve a certain detached impartiality. . . . [A person] will think ineffectively in the degree in which his preferences modify the stuff of his observations and reasonings. . . . The value of the reflection lies upon keeping one's self out of the data." [18]

[17] Ibid., p. 228. See also How We Think, p. 141.
[18] Democracy and Education, p. 173.

Likewise the following passage comports ill with the view that the object of (philosophic) knowledge is " a living picture of the choice of thoughtful men about what they would have life to be ":

It is one thing to say that all knowing has an end beyond itself, and another thing, a thing of a contrary kind, to say that an act of knowing has a particular end which it is bound, in advance, to reach. Much less is it true that the instrumental nature of thinking means that it exists for the sake of obtaining some private one-sided advantage upon which one has set one's heart.[19]

So far is it from being the case that philosophy's concern with social ethics renders metaphysical inquiry vain and useless, that we now find that the possession of a valid metaphysics is the first prerequisite for an enlightened practice. Our beliefs about the nature of existence must inevitably play a major rôle in determining how we should live our lives:

The more sure one is that the world which encompasses human life is of such and such a character (no matter what his definition), the more one is committed to try to direct the conduct of life, that of others as well as of himself, upon the basis of the character assigned to the world.[20]

These passages, then, are manifestly irreconcilable with those which preceded. Philosophy cannot be concerned, on the one hand, solely with moral ends and the means to their attainment—be, in other words, merely an enlightened social ethics; and, on the other hand, have a place for metaphysics, which, if it is at all possible, must deal with the traits of existence as they are in themselves, uncolored by the ethical views of the metaphysician. What

[19] *Reconstruction in Philosophy,* p. 146.
[20] *Experience and Nature,* pp. 413-4.

has led Dewey to argue in behalf of two such contradictory theses? A partial explanation will be found in the fact that he occasionally falls into the " genetic " fallacy, and contends that, because man's interest in metaphysics has a " moral " background, the philosopher cannot construct valid formulations of the characters and relations of the items of any Reality which is conceived as independent of man and his problems. All such constructions are mere " wish-fulfillments " or, in his words, *nothing but* " living pictures of the choice of thoughtful men about what they would have life to be." A far more basic and subtle confusion has its origin in a valuable discovery which Dewey has made about the procedure of traditional metaphysicians. He charges that while they were ostensibly engaged in a search for ultimate reality, they were concerned, for the most part, to conserve values, and that because of this bias they illicitly converted a moral ideal into a metaphysics of existence.

" Reality " as the object of philosophic research is described with the properties required by the choice of good that has occurred.[21]

In briefest formula, " reality " becomes what we wish existence to be, after we have analyzed its defects and decided upon what would remove them; " reality " is what existence would be if our reasonably justified preferences were so completely established in nature as to exhaust and define its entire being and thereby render search and struggle unnecessary.[22]

Traditional philosophers have thus affirmed the reality *par excellence* of those traits of existence which satisfy the moral demand. They have chiefly insisted upon stability and permanence, largely because the actual world furnishes so few examples of things that are either permanent

[21] *Experience and Nature* (1st ed.), p. 34.
[22] *Ibid.*, pp. 53-4.

or stable. This conversion of " the *reflective* idea of the good . . . into a norm and model of being " Dewey has labelled " *the* philosophic fallacy." [23]

Whether Dewey's charge concerning the procedure of traditional metaphysicians is true as a generalization is open to some question, but the ethical motivation of the doctrine of many illustrious philosophers is unmistakable.[24] Dewey avoids this confusion by drawing a distinction between philosophy and metaphysics. Philosophy is defined as the love of wisdom, concerned with prudence and the generation and maintenance of goods. Metaphysics, on the other hand, is the study of the generic traits of existence. As a psychological fact, man is naturally philosophical, not coldly metaphysical. He is not engaged in the bare noting of existential characters and their relations one to another, but is interested rather in their bearing upon the good life. The task of philosophy, therefore, is not *completed* by the construction of a metaphysics. This once accomplished, to be truly philosophical, we must see what our metaphysics exacts of us in behavior and belief.

All this is both sane and intelligible. One cannot but think that Dewey has forgotten his own analysis in the passages, already quoted, which deny in effect that philosophy can include metaphysics. It is the writer's belief that Dewey was led to make these incautious statements in reaction against the invalid procedure of earlier thinkers.

---

[23] *Ibid.,* pp. 34, 35.

[24] A contemporary champion of the doctrine which Dewey is criticizing is Professor Wilbur Urban. In his *The Intelligible World,* he argues at length that metaphysics has been—and should be—inseparably bound up with the problem of values. "The inseparability of value and reality is the one constant character of the intelligible world, and a world in which they are divorced would no longer be intelligible." *Ibid.,* p. 178.

In emphasizing his opposition to what he considered the traditional standpoint, he denied too much—or more, at least, than was necessary for his purpose. Dewey's frequent exhortations that philosophers eschew metaphysics and deal exclusively with the human significance of events are thus supported more by conviction than by argument. The philosopher may legitimately continue to exercise both of these functions, and Dewey himself recognizes this truth except when essentially irrelevant considerations enter his mind. When philosophers who are primarily interested in the second function overhastily transfer considerations appropriate to it to their discussion of the first, they commit the fallacy which Dewey has justly pointed out. The study of existence must inevitably be vitiated, if value considerations are allowed to intrude; but our knowledge of existence can and should be applied to the furtherance of the actual production of values.

CHAPTER X

INFLUENCE OF EDUCATIONAL THEORY UPON DEWEY'S PHILOSOPHY

Dewey's theory of knowledge has developed from a starting point essentially different from the usual one. Most epistemologies presume certain cases of knowledge or supposed knowledge, and then proceed to scrutinize the nature and validity of the cognitive claim, asking, " What can we know? " and " How can we know? " His educational interests early swerved him away from this procedure, and impelled him to raise a different type of question. Instead of assuming knowledge as an attained goal and investigating its character, he asks what methods we employ in getting knowledge. What is the nature of inquiry? Through what processes do we *arrive at* an assertion of knowledge? Certain terminological peculiarities of Dewey's epistemology are also rendered intelligible once their educational background is recognized.

Dewey states that the end and aim of education is· " *the formation of careful, alert, and thorough habits of thinking.*" [1]

It is [the business of education] to cultivate deep-seated and effective habits of discriminating tested beliefs from mere assertions, guesses, and opinions; to develop a lively, sincere, and open-minded preference for conclusions that are properly grounded, and to ingrain into the individual's working habits, *methods of inquiry and reasoning appropriate to the various problems that present themselves.*[2]

As intelligence is operative only in the settling of problems, it can reach its fullest development only by being

[1] *How We Think,* p. 58.
[2] *Ibid.,* pp. 27-8. Italics mine. See also p. 168.

presented with situations which raise them. " Effective and integral thinking is possible only where the experimental method in some form is used." [3]

This thesis of Dewey's implies more, however, than a criticism of older theories of education; it amounts to a new theory about learning. Learning is concerned solely with the novel. The familiar, well-worn path presents no difficulties and does not challenge thought; nor is intelligence or reflection involved in the recognition of that which has once been learnt:

Ideas may lose their intellectual quality as they are habitually used. . . . [In familiar objects] the thing and the meaning are so completely fused that there is no judgment and no idea proper, but only automatic recognition.[4]

To speak of the passing attention which a traveler has occasionally to give to the indications of his proper path in a fairly familiar and beaten highway as knowledge, in just the same sense in which the deliberate inquiry of a mathematician or a chemist or a logician is knowledge, is as confusing to the real issue involved as would be the denial to it of *any* reflective factor.[5]

In modern science, learning is finding out what nobody has previously known. It is a transaction in which nature is teacher, and in which the teacher comes to knowledge and truth only through the learning of the inquiring student.[6]

But what of the many cases in which some fact or series of facts is well established? Is there no intelligible sense in which the acquisition of this information can be called learning? Dewey does not deny this possibility, but lays down one important condition: the student must be able to rethink afresh the problem out of which the knowledge

---

[3] *Ibid.*, p. 99.   [5] *Essays in Experimental Logic*, p. 245.
[4] *Ibid.*, p. 110.   [6] *Experience and Nature*, p. 152.

of these facts emerged and must perceive the bearings which it has upon the solution. " Originality means personal interest in the question, personal initiative in turning over suggestions furnished by others, and sincerity in following them out to a tested conclusion."[7] That this is both a true and important observation about educational technique will scarcely be questioned now. In contrast with the older method of mere memorization and recitation, in which the material to be learned remained " external " to the mind of the pupil, the newer method provides for a genuine assimilation of the new material and at the same time tends to develop the student's mental powers and vision.

The bearing of all this upon epistemology does not become completely evident until we follow the next step in Dewey's reasoning. " Knowing " is now identified with learning, and " knowledge " means that information which is acquired as a result of reflective inquiry.

Knowledge is an affair of *making* sure, not of grasping antecedently given sureties.[8]

The static, cold-storage ideal of knowledge is inimical to educative development. . . . It swamps thinking.[9]

Taking what is already known or pointing to it is no more a case of knowledge than taking a chisel out of a tool box is the making of the tool.[10]

It is important to bear these and similar passages in mind, since they define the terminology without which Dewey's subsequent arguments cannot be understood. " Knowledge " does not mean the awareness or statement of a fact. Even though a person may be able to recall

[7] *How We Think*, p. 198. [9] *Democracy and Education*, p. 186.
[8] *Experience and Nature*, p. 154. [10] *The Quest for Certainty*, p. 188.

thousands of actual events and state their manifold relations to one another with complete accuracy, he cannot be
said to " know " them, in Dewey's sense, unless he had
some purposive part in the production of the original
knowledge of them. The mere accumulation of information, e. g., by reading accounts in histories, is not a case
of knowing. Dewey is not unaware of the wide divergence between his use of the term " knowledge " and its
traditional and current usage. He relates the two in the
following manner:

" Knowledge," in the sense of information, means the working
capital, the indispensable resources, of further inquiry; of finding out, or learning, more things.[11]

What is already *known*, what is accepted as truth, is of immense
importance; inquiry could not proceed a step without it.   But
it is held subject to use, and is at the mercy of the discoveries
which it makes possible.[12]

His view finds perhaps its clearest expression in these
passages:

When the thing of which we are now retrospectively aware was
in process of being known, it was prospective and eventual to
inquiry, not something already " given."   And it has *cognitive*
force in a new inquiry whose objective and ultimate object is
now prospective.[13]

So far as it is already certain that this *is* ice, and also certain
that ice, under all circumstances cools water, the meaning-rela-
tion stands on the same level as the physical, being not merely
suggested, but part of the facts ascertained.   It is not a meaning-
relation as such at all.   We already have truth; the entire work
of knowing as logical is done; we have no longer the relation

---

[11] *Democracy and Education*, pp. 185-6.
[12] *Experience and Nature*, p. 154. My italics.
[13] *The Quest for Certainty*, p. 188.

characteristic of reflective situations. . . . The problem of valid determination remains the central question of any theory of knowing in its relation to facts and truth.[14]

Dewey's preoccupation with learning and inquiry in dealing with epistemological matters crops out in his protest against the platform of the " new realists." The vital problem ignored by them is " that of getting knowledge, of passing from doubt and guesswork to grounded conclusions." [15] He puts the question, " Is logic primarily an account of *getting* knowledge, with a concept of achieved knowledge serving only as a limiting term, or is it a theory of knowledge *achieved?* " [16] As Dewey states it elsewhere, " The decisive consideration as between instrumentalism and analytic realism is whether the operation of experimentation is or is not necessary to knowledge. The instrumental theory holds that it is." [17]

It is their failure to recognize the central position of inquiry that has, Dewey thinks, led the usual varieties of epistemology astray. In any truly cognitive situation—so runs the argument—present data are interpreted as suggesting external, not-present existents and their relations. The presented phenomena serve as *evidence*. But the operations of inference and prediction must include a *manipulation* of the data—else the experience is not

---

[14] *Essays in Experimental Logic*, p. 236. The motivation of Dewey's reasoning on this point, is, in part, clearly educational in origin. It is not sufficient to point to any one's *ipse dixit*, whether he be a teacher or any other repository of authority, to validate the assertion of a particular bit of information. The student must be able to show by what methods it has been ascertained. Although this need not be done in every case, and would be, in fact, impossible in actual practice, a procedure is furnished by which any particular item of knowledge—if called into question—may be tested.

[15] *Journal of Philosophy, etc.*, VII (1910), 556.

[16] *Ibid.*, p. 557.

[17] *Essays in Experimental Logic*, p. 32.

properly cognitive. It follows that bare statements of fact are not, strictly speaking, propositions, nor does the mere " mental " representation of a non-present existent constitute a genuine " idea." [18] It can be seen that such a view requires a wholesale revision of the usual terms of epistemological and logical discourse, and Dewey does not hesitate to make this demand explicit:

Does not an account of thinking, basing itself on modern scientific procedure, demand a statement in which all the distinctions and terms of thought—judgment, concept, inference, subject, predicate, and copula of judgment, etc., *ad infinitum*—shall be interpreted simply and entirely as distinctive functions or divisions of labor within the doubt-inquiry process? [19]

Dewey's major problem, then, is to give " an account of intellectual operations and conditions from the standpoint of the rôle played and position occupied by them in the business of drawing inferences." [20] From this position two conclusions are drawn. First, traditional theories pay too little attention to the functional aspects of thinking. Too much praise cannot be given Dewey for supplying the needed corrective; he has shown conclusively that

---

[18] " Ideas are not . . . genuine ideas unless they are tools in a reflective examination which tends to solve a problem. Suppose it is a question of having the pupil grasp *the idea* of the sphericity of the earth. This is different from teaching him its sphericity *as a fact.* . . . To grasp sphericity as an idea, the pupil must first have realized certain perplexities or confusing features in observed facts and have had the idea of spherical shape suggested to him as a possible way of accounting for the phenomena in question. Only by use as a method of interpreting data so as to give them fuller meaning does sphericity become a genuine idea. There may be a vivid image and no idea; or there may be a fleeting, obscure image and yet an idea, *if that image performs the function of instigating and directing the observation and relation of facts.*" *How We Think*, p. 109. Last italics mine.

[19] *Essays in Experimental Logic*, p. 219.

[20] *Ibid.*, p. 220. See also p. 134.

man's logical and cognitive activity does not take place in an intellectual vacuum, but plays an indispensable part in the business of living. His findings in this field supplement the work of more conventional logicians and epistemologists, and clarify the latter's observations by placing them in their proper context.[21] The second inference is destructive and attempts to demonstrate the actual invalidity of the traditional conception of formal logic. Dewey offers an alternative interpretation of various cognitive phenomena, and at the same time contends that the meaning which he assigns to various terms of logic is the only correct one. But is this contention sound? Dr. Joseph Ratner has elaborated Dewey's thesis in a paper [22] which merits close analysis, both because of the seriousness of its charges against traditional logic and of the boldness with which its author makes explicit some of the bizarre implications of Dewey's epistemology.

Dr. Ratner's argument may be summarized in six propositions: (a) Logic properly deals with inquiry, with the process of judging which eventuates in the *assertion of knowledge*. (b) The proposition must be considered " in

[21] Because of the revised terminology which Dewey employs, many of his statements take on the air of paradoxes and tend, consequently, to confuse his readers, when they are more truly tautological, following directly from his definitions. Thus his oft-debated statement that facts and meanings change in inquiry appears at first sight to ascribe an intolerable elusiveness and slipperiness to existence. You cannot rely, it would seem, upon a thing to be definitely this or that—even at a given time; for whenever an attempt is made to know what it is, it by that act changes its characters. But actually nothing of the sort is implied. "Fact" just means what is accepted as assured in a given inquiry, and the " meaning " of a concept is, for Dewey, *what it suggests in a specific investigation*; and the variability of *such* facts and meanings is obvious.

[22] " John Dewey's Theory of Judgment," *Journal of Philosophy*, XXVII (1930), 253 ff. Dewey says of this paper, " in his [Ratner's] case a sympathetic understanding is manifest which calls for no reply." *Ibid.*, p. 277.

relation to the process of inquiry of which it is a terminus." (c) In this process—as Dewey analyzes it—
are: i. a problem set in non-cognitive experience; ii. the
process of judging (which alone is cognitive); and iii.
the solution, which is non-cognitive also. " The proposition which is the terminus of the process of judgment
belongs to the third non-cognitive phase. And, therefore,
it falls outside judgment proper." [23] (d) The apprehension of such a proposition is, therefore, not a case of
" knowledge." (e) Such propositions cannot be " true "
or " false." (f) Only hypothetical propositions can be
true or false. Dr. Ratner concludes that the whole trouble
with traditional logic lies in the failure of its practitioners
to consider the nature of inquiry. " The practice of treating the conclusion *of* inquiry, independent of any context
as the beginning *for* inquiry, of treating isolated termini
of the process of judgment, as the original subject-matter
for judgment this practice is indeed the basic confusion
of this logic—if we may single out one confusion as being
more basic than another." [24]

Let us take up these points in turn. The first does not
require separate discussion, since, unless it can be shown
that other studies which have gone under the name of
logic are invalid, the issue is solely one of terminology.
Ratner's second contention, which is apparently inspired
by the organismic dialectic, involves a real issue. It implies that every characteristic and attribute of propositions
is conditioned by the circumstance that they are asserted
at the end of inquiries. But to those who do not accept
the premise of the internality of all relations *that* is a
proposition requiring proof, and it is not to be proved
by a mere reassertion of the disputed premise. It is not

[23] *Ibid.*, p. 260.   [24] *Ibid.*, p. 261.

denied that the first categorical assertion of a proposition occurs only at the end of inquiry—after it has been tested as thoroughly as possible. But the proposition may be held tentatively, pending inquiry, and its form is the same, *so far as its relation to the existential state of affairs which it symbolizes is concerned,* as that of the proposition asserted categorically. In the one case we say, " probably A is B, or probably xRy " instead of "A is B, xRy." In both cases certain characters or relations are attributed to existential subject-matter, and the only difference between the two consists in our mental attitude towards what is asserted.

Does, then, confusion result from the fact that formal logicians take the " proposition " as the beginning of inquiry? This conclusion follows only if position-in-inquiry is relevant to the problems which they investigate—a condition which does not, in fact, exist. Formal logic has nothing to say about the truth or falsity of isolated propositions. It is concerned with the structure of propositions which makes inference possible. It shows us how from the truth of certain propositions we can pass to the truth or falsity of others without carrying on any additional investigations beyond those required to establish the first. Similarly, the observed falsity of certain propositions can serve as the basis for the assertion of other propositions which bear the required formal relations to the first. More generally,

the principles of logic state the general conditions under which the truth or falsity of certain propositions would determine the truth or falsity of certain others, and thus permit us (if we wished to do so) to draw correct inferences. . . . Logical principles are therefore truths concerning the possible relationships of certain (possible) objects of our thought, and they are grounded in the nature of these objects, not in the nature of our thinking psychologically considered.[25]

The method of formal logic is not the method of scientific inquiry, and no absurdity could be greater than to maintain that it is.[26] But the employment of logical principles is an integral part—even in Dewey's own theory— of the technique of scientific investigation—either in revealing latent inconsistencies or in elaborating consequences which may be empirically verified. It is likewise true that the principles of logic, taken by themselves, are incapable of demonstrating a single metaphysical theorem; and if such philosophers as certain new realists at one extreme, or Hegel and the panlogists at the other, have appeared to reason thus, they have been enabled to do so only by means of an additional implicit disputable premise as to the nature of existence. With such aberrations and unwarranted claims eliminated, there remains to formal logic, both in its theoretical and its practical aspects, a position of importance as a subject of human inquiry.[27]

Ratner's next contention is that assertoric propositions are not properly termed cases of knowledge at all:

We would be totally unworthy of the spirit his [Dewey's] philosophy inspires, if we did not have the courage to say that the

[25] R. M. Eaton, *General Logic,* New York, Scribner's, 1931, p. 7. The first chapter of this book is an excellent discussion of the general nature of logic.

[26] It is not inconsistent with this statement to assert that as a science advances, its propositions tend to fit more and more into the framework of a deductive system.

[27] This brief statement is not offered as a conclusive demonstration that formal logic is either a useful or valid inquiry. Such a demonstration would require an elaborate discussion outside the scope of this work. It does show why the charge of confusion is unfounded.

immediate intellectual apprehension of propositions is no more than the immediate sensory perception of sense-data, a case of knowledge . . . We do *not* know propositions taken individually and in isolation from their functional context—*i. e.,* in their immediate relation to the mind; what we *do* know are propositions taken together in their relationships to one another and to the context in which their evidential value is developed and used—*i. e.,* we know propositions in their mediate relation to the mind.[28]

This passage is not entirely free from confusion itself, for Ratner tends to identify the " immediate " with the " isolated " character of propositions. This is evident from the analogy which he draws between them and sense-data. Pure sensory awareness is rightly said to be non-cognitive, for—in so far as it is infallible—it gives evidence only of its own transient existence. Therefore, if by the " immediate apprehension of a proposition " is meant merely the fact of its assertion, the parallel between it and sensory awareness is complete. But just as evanescent sensa may suggest, stand for, " represent," continuing objects, so propositions—when their " meaning " and not their bare existence is considered—symbolize states of affairs which may or may not be the case. When the proposition represents what is actually the case, it is ordinarily said to be true; otherwise, it is false. It may be true in isolation from other propositions because its truth or falsity is dependent solely upon the existence of the facts referred to. This is a perfectly intelligible sense in which propositions can be said to be " true " or " false," although Ratner (following Dewey) may protest that it is not a fruitful or convenient way of defining these properties.[29] If this point is well taken, nothing

[28] *Loc. cit.,* pp. 259-60.
[29] Because of the failure to accept the Deweyan identification of " truth "

remains of Ratner's argument except certain verbal propositions derived from Dewey's redefinition of " knowledge " and " cognitive." In Dewey's sense of these terms, assertoric propositions do not make up the body of " knowledge," nor is man performing a " cognitive " function when he holds them " before the mind." But these definitions can solve no empirical problems concerning matters of fact—no matter how often or how resolutely they are reiterated. The *validity* of the traditional use of these terms remains unimpaired. It is evident, then, that whereas Dewey's studies in logical theory have been of great significance on their positive side, particularly in relation to problems of educational theory, his belief that they invalidate the older logic is mistaken. This error has come about because the preponderance of Dewey's attention has been directed to the functional aspects of thinking, to the neglect of *what* that thought is *of*.

and " verification." According to the present view, these are separable properties of propositions. Truth is a property of the relation between the proposition and the fact it signifies. Verification necessitates an additional relation of implication between the original proposition and auxiliary propositions, which are capable of direct testing. Thus, as Ratner says, a hypothetical proposition must be taken in its functional context before it can be *verified*. But it must be repeated that such indirect verification cannot be a complete guarantor of the truth of the original proposition, although the more frequently it is verified the more confident we shall be that it is true.

CHAPTER XI

CONCLUSION

Now that we approach the end of our task, the question may well be asked, what is the significance of such a study? Although no attempt has been made to give a final evaluation of Dewey's philosophy, the essential basis for such an estimate should be provided in this essay; for no criticism of Dewey's philosophy as a whole can pretend to be valid unless it is founded upon such a discrimination of the various strains in his thought. Besides furnishing this necessary prolegomenon to any definitive study of Dewey, the present work has established two important points.

(1) An enormous complexity of factors is involved in Dewey's discussion of any specific philosophical issue. No particular movement ("pragmatism," "immediate empiricism," or "empirical naturalism") can be said to represent a single attitude or method in philosophy, if Dewey is to be identified with it. For through all his work there runs a complex, interrelated, yet often incongruous set of motivations, the net result of which is that he can seldom stand unambiguously and unequivocally on one side of any important philosophical controversy. It would be well, therefore, if partisans of Dewey, instead of giving a blanket indorsement of his views under the name of, say, "instrumentalism," were to state specifically which of the foregoing premises or motivations of the compound so designated they are in sympathy with and are prepared to defend. By what may be termed an historical accident (subjection to the particular influences which have been enumerated) Dewey has combined into one philosophy a diverse set of principles which are not

113

completely congruous with one another and are even in some cases contradictory; and it is not likely that any of Dewey's followers would be prepared to adopt these *in toto*. The cause of specificity in philosophical discussion has been furthered by the enumeration of the complete list of tendencies presented in this essay; and this should facilitate any subsequent consideration of them.

(2) Most readers when making their first acquaintance with Dewey's writings are frequently puzzled by apparent inconsistencies and contradictions in his text—contradictions which may appear on the same or adjacent pages of a particular discussion; and he also, perhaps more than any other contemporary philosopher, employs a vocabulary in which the terms vary considerably in meaning in the same or related discussions. This is due to his unusual sensitiveness to diverse considerations when engaged in the analysis of a particular problem. As he writes rather facilely, there is often no clear indication to the reader (nor sometimes, it would appear, to himself) that he has passed from one type of consideration to a second which may not be compatible with the first. It is hoped that the present work will serve to put the reader on his guard for such shifts in points-of-view, and for the alterations in the meaning of terms which sometimes follow from them.

The first point may be illustrated by a few examples. Dewey, it has been shown, appeals on numerous occasions to the principles of " creative novelty " and " continuity." Now these two principles, when generalized, have a contrary significance for metaphysics. Is the universe " all of a piece," in which a fundamental unity of character and function can be discerned? Or is it essentially pluralistic, heterogeneous, ever introducing novel types of existents and exhibiting diversity of function? As one embraces the one or the other alternative the character of his basic metaphysical allegiance is determined. This fact is abundantly illustrated in the history of philosophy. Yet Dewey, as this essay has shown, tries to answer both questions in the affirmative. But is this possible without falling into contradiction? And if formal contradiction is avoidable, does not Dewey's attempt to reap the benefits of both points of view compel him to give fundamentally different and incongruous solutions of particular problems? That this is indeed the case may be indicated briefly as follows: One problem discussed by Dewey is the proper interpretation of intelligence *as a function.* Following the *reductive* [1] method, intelligence is considered as a function which has developed as an aid to biological survival. It is then " reduced " to an instrument of biological advancement, presumably a favorable variation which has persisted.[2] Opposed to this is the view of " creative novelty." Intelligence is a distinctive function, novel in character, not explicable on biological principles and not describable by biological laws. These are two irreconcilable accounts of the nature of intelligence, the second finally gaining the upper hand in Dewey.[3] Let us turn to another aspect of the question does the entrance of intelligence into nature mark the

[1] As Professor Lovejoy has pointed out in " The Meanings of Emergence and its Modes," *Journal of Philosophical Studies,* II (1927), 167 ff., the principle of continuity may be applied to a causal sequence in one of two ways, the *reductive* or the *retrotensive.* The former seeks to describe the later events in the sequence by the same categories that are applicable to a description of the events in the earlier phase. The latter attempts to read back into the earlier phase of the process the supposedly emergent characters of the later phase.

[2] See Chapter IV. This, it is granted, is a minor point in Dewey.

[3] In spite of this Dewey (and Professor Mead) continued to draw certain negative conclusions as to what thought could do from the premise that intelligence was merely an aid to action. See above, p. 41.

appearance of *new types of entities* as well as of behavior? When Dewey was influenced by the reductive
ideal, he asserted, as we have seen, a kind of behaviorism
which limits all novelty to modes of behavior and denies
that any existential emergence is implied by the entrance
of mind upon the cosmic scene.[4] Yet it was also observed,
contrary to this, that when Dewey studied the situation
in which intelligence operates, he asserted that an essential condition for successful forecast is the occurrence of
that novel and apparently unique kind of existence of
objects signified by the terms " presence-as-absence " or
" vicarious existence." No one supposes physical objects
to be endowed with such a property; yet Dewey offers no
satisfactory account of the proper relation between these
at least *prima facie* different types of existents.

An analogous divergence in the interpretation of time
and the temporal process follows from the adoption
of the one or the other principle. The principle of continuity, in its reductive form, has been combined with the
principle of determinacy to form a basic postulate of
natural science [5]: that time is a mere vehicle for the
rearrangement of pre-existent entities in accordance with
laws constant throughout all phases of the process. It has
always been a prime motive with Dewey to make his
philosophy thoroughly " scientific " in character, and it
would appear surprising that this line of thought has not
been developed, were it not that another conception of
time is much more congenial to him. He abhors the
thought of a " block universe," whether of the mechan-

---

[4] It was when he was guided by this line of thought that Dewey
attempted to reduce meanings to language behavior plus other bodily adjustments, or to a relation between purely physical events.

[5] It is not implied that the principle of continuity is a necessary pre-
supposition of science.

istic or the absolutistic type; and a radical metaphysical indeterminism marks much of his work. It is reasonable to conjecture that his unwillingness to admit this logical implication of the reductive premise has occasioned his shift to the "retrotensive" method of interpreting the principle of continuity.

After this shift occurs, the principle of continuity no longer makes it necessary to deny existence to, or assert the illusory nature of, the empirical traits of human experience; the problem now becomes, as we have seen, that of reading back into pre-human existence the characters which are ordinarily attributed to distinctively human experience. Dewey merely asserts the bare possibility of a solution of this sort, without attempting to work it out in any detail. We may, indeed, confidently declare that he merely brings the retrotensive method forward so that he can accept without discount the manifold and diverse characters of the vital and the mental and still pay lip service to the principle of continuity with its associated denial of bifurcation. We should expect the formulation of some type of panpsychist theory (as the previous quotation from Woodbridge and the passages in Dewey's writings upon which it is based indicate),[6] but there is ample reason why this tendency should remain submerged in Dewey's "subconscious." For panpsychism is just as incompatible with his favorite thesis of creative novelty as any mechanistic theory could be. Intelligence, according to that theory, would not mark the occurrence in nature of an essentially new type of happening; and emotions and thought, instead of constituting a new level of existence, would have to be read back in some manner as traits of previous groupings of events (or objects).

[6] See Chapter VIII.

9

There is not and cannot be, therefore, at least in so far as Dewey's philosophy represents such an attempt, a consistent conjunction of the two principles of continuity and creative novelty; and the adherence to either compels the denial of the characteristic theses of the other.

Another pair of principles which Dewey holds, but which tend to contrary conclusions, are the two varieties of empiricism which were distinguished. When he is dominated by the " immediate empiricist " strain, Dewey gives one account of the fundamental character of reality and knowledge; when influenced by " objective " or scientific empiricism, he gives a radically different account. Dewey in his " immediate empiricist " mood is concerned mainly with the richness and diversity of the qualities given in non-reflective awareness. At such times, he feels that it is experiences of this kind, those of pure esthesis, which acquaint us with the true nature of reality. Passage after passage has been cited [7] which asserts that this type of experience is preëminently fitted to disclose the real. But, as we have repeated, perhaps *ad nauseam,* the fact of knowledge has bulked large in Dewey's thought, and man in his *cognitive* capacity seems to affirm the existence of a world quite other in its characters and in its laws from that which is directly experienced—a world from which all disorder, warmth, color and poignancy have been purged.[8] Dewey finds himself unable to give " full faith and credit " to this world which cognition reveals; for knowledge, as he conceives it, is essentially mediate in character, always transcending the bare given, and is,

[7] See above, pp. 21 ff.

[8] There have been some late developments in the philosophy of science which have a contrary effect, but these were too recent to influence Dewey's reasoning on this point. He has used them since to justify the position which he had already adopted.

therefore, constitutionally defective as an instrument for revealing reality. Nor could he take the easy course of partitioning existence into two realms—one disclosed by cognition and the other disclosed by immediate experience—because this solution would run contrary to the principle of continuity and to his general bias against dualism. Darwinism, with its negative thesis concerning knowledge, here comes to his aid.[9] If knowledge is conceived merely as an aid to survival, without power to disclose any characters of reality as such, the problem of reconciling objects of knowledge and those of immediate experience vanishes. Phenomenalism supplemented by a fictional account of scientific concepts seems to be the logical outcome of this way of thinking. These doctrines, after being almost wholly submerged in *Experience and Nature,* again come nearly to the fore in *The Quest for Certainty.* It is this subjectivistic strain in Dewey, a survival from his early idealism, that leads him to magnify the rôle of immediate experience in reality. Science, which allegedly deals with a world independent of, and qualitatively different from, the data of immediate experience, deals actually with fictions, pure creations of the mind, whose only justification or validity is their ability to enrich non-cognitive experience.

Objective or scientific empiricism has very different philosophic consequences. It starts out with the conception of man as primarily an organism. Both he and the experience associated with his peculiar stage of develop-

[9] This thesis, in its strict form, has always appeared to the present writer a patent self-contradiction. It is openly realistic in its assumption of biological evolution and in its belief that we are acquainted with the circumstances surrounding the origin and growth of intelligence. It then asserts that intelligence is *solely* a biological function, deserts realism, and restricts the meaning of propositions to their significance for survival.

ment are late comers in the world. This habitat, which had long preëxisted man's arrival and will doubtless outlast him countless eons, can, however, disclose itself only through his experience. The ordinary realistic view holds that the state of nature prior to the emergence of man and his experience is a transempirical fact which can be conceived only by means of a mental extrapolation from present experienceable sequences of natural events. In Dewey's objectivistic interpretation of " experience," that term denotes the complete situation in which the organism is functioning—a situation capable of indefinite elasticity—stretching back into the remote past and forward into the distant future. So long as the event (or object) has any causal relation to the agent's present activity it is " in experience," nor is consciousness of such an event a necessary condition for its being in experience. It, therefore, like the transempirical object of the realist, must be reconstructed by means of inference. The methods of scientific inquiry alone are capable of determining the proper characters to be assigned these bygone existents which are no longer open to direct inspection. Whether we call the whole process " experience " or not is immaterial provided we recognize that it is by means of the present *directly* experienceable data and certain hypotheses concerning uniformities of relational connection that the process is capable of being intellectually grasped. Dewey's conception here is essentially realistic.[10] But science in its dealings with present entities and events which are not open to direct inspection (*e. g.,* because of their minuteness) follows substantially the same procedure as in its reconstruction of past events. The im-

---

[10] See the introductory chapter to the 2nd ed. of *Experience and Nature.* Dewey assumes also that the retrotensive form of the principle of continuity is a valid methodological postulate for this construction.

perceptible events are so conceived as to fit into a coherent scheme with the data of experience. Dewey's empiricist craving seems at times to be satisfied if the existence of scientific objects is indirectly verified in immediate experience. Such a demand, however, the most extreme realist would hardly deny. No one would be concerned to assert the existence of hypothetical entities or processes if they did not serve to " explain " the occurrence of sensory data; but in order to function as links in the chain of perceptible events, the entities of science must be actual substantive existents, and not bare relational qualities, as Dewey sometimes seems to suggest—the interaction of mere relations could not conceivably give birth to any perceptual object. But once a fictional account, concerned with prediction only, is given up, these scientific entities must be thought of as possessing the characters (or lack of them) which science asserts. Science is not opposed to the postulational technique. Its life-blood is hypothesis, and it owes its fruitfulness to its temerity in going beyond the immediate data of experience and constructing entities to suit its purposes. The only limitation scientific empiricism imposes is that these entities be defined in such a way that a method is furnished for testing them in immediate experience. As long as such verification is indirect, it is necessarily incomplete. To assert a complete verification would obviously be fallacious (" the affirmation of the consequent ") ; but science assumes that various types of indirect verification lend great probability to the truth of its hypotheses, and in this claim nature seems to bear it out.

We have recited these commonplaces of scientific method for this reason: since Dewey uses the blanket term " empiricism " for the two different tendencies we have been noting, he confuses one tendency with, or

122   THE PHILOSOPHY OF JOHN DEWEY

illicitly substitutes each in turn for, the other. To be a scientific empiricist is equivalent to limiting oneself to the assertion of propositions the implications of which are verifiable in immediate perceptual experience. But Dewey goes on to give, in the name of science, that fundamentally distorted and paradoxical account of judgment which was analyzed in Chapters V and VI.[11] When the practical strain is dominant, he tells us that only future *acts* and their perceptible consequences can be judged; when practice is not so urgent, references, to be valid, need only be to future elements of non-reflective experience. These contentions were carefully examined, and we need merely repeat the conclusion of those discussions: that, in his treatment of this subject, Dewey misrepresents both the psychological and the logical situation involved in judgment. It appears, then, that Dewey's empiricisms are incapable of forming a genuine synthesis, tending to contrary conclusions as soon as their implications are drawn.

It was shown in Chapter I how radically opposed the totalistic and particularistic interpretations of the organismic dialectic are. The former leads to absolutism; the latter implies the most extreme form of relativism. According to the first nothing is wholly real but the absolute totality, and no complete truth is possible except from the standpoint of the whole; according to the second it is individual standpoints and perspectives which are the sole marks of the real, and not only are meaning and truth conditioned by perspectives, but these concepts are definable only in terms of standpoints.[12] Professor Love-

[11] Particularly pp. 52 ff. and 61 ff.
[12] Of course, only a vestige of the totalistic interpretation has survived in Dewey's thought—when he discusses the limited contexts in which reflective inquiry takes place.

joy has contrasted Dewey's immediate empiricism and his emphasis upon the practical character of intelligence.[13] The latter, he finds, has definitely realistic implications; the former, as we have seen, tends to phenomenalism. That the doctrine of organism is fundamentally incompatible with temporalism has also been suggested in the text [14] this could be shown in much greater detail. It is not our purpose, however, to belabor all the inconsistencies in Dewey's writings.

Just as opposing principles abound in Dewey, others form definitely coherent groups. These latter are more apparent, however, and need not be exhibited at length. Emergence or creative novelty is, for example, an extreme form of temporalism; and practicalism is a species of futurism with an additional emphasis upon acts or operations. Practicalism is the hybrid offspring of Darwinism and immediate empiricism. The relationship can be shown in this fashion. Darwinism, because of its insistence upon function, must take note of a temporal continuum which contains the conditions of the act, the act, and the consequences of the act. But immediate empiricism is a dialectic of the instantaneous, which will have nothing to do with a real temporal spread of events of which some are unexperienced or unexperienceable. The total emphasis is then laid upon future acts and practical consequences; for they, while " practical," are also presumably capable of being experienced.

The notion of creative intelligence was partly an outgrowth of Darwinism, although in its final form it had to deny the negative thesis inherent in that doctrine. To

---

[13] D. Drake, A. O. Lovejoy and others, *Essays in Critical Realism,* New York, Macmillan, 1920, pp. 76-81.

[14] Above p. 135.

assert the efficacy of intelligence, Dewey had to relate it to the other biological functions from which it developed; but to establish its emergent character, he had to surrender his earlier belief that intelligence was *solely* a biological function (which is the Darwinian thesis). Also Darwinism itself is largely but an application of the organismic logic to a limited context. The doctrine of organism implies that a given entity cannot be adequately described without placing it in its total context. Darwinism is less exacting in its demands, requiring the consideration of but a small contextual situation of origin and function. Except, moreover, for the fact that the term "biology" or one of its derivatives is usually employed when the method of Darwinism is invoked, the distinction between the two doctrines is very tenuous indeed. Nor is this at all surprising when it is considered that the introduction of the biological interpretation of intelligence marked the passage from the totalistic to the particularistic interpretation of the doctrine of organism. That doctrine was merely transformed, not abandoned; and it must be confessed that when Dewey is advocating the "genetic" or "functional" method, it is not always clear whether he is thinking of Darwinism, "organism," or both. Some of the quotations which were utilized to illustrate the one doctrine could have been transferred to illustrate the other without loss of accuracy.

Educational theory is a field in which the practical character of intelligence is capable of clear exhibition. Except as it reacts upon his epistemology and thus becomes interrelated with the doctrine of organism, it has no close affinity with any of the other tendencies which have been outlined. "Moralism" is closely bound up with the principles of creative intelligence, organism and continuity. First, the moral judgment is a particular case of the practical judgment. In the second place, all moral situations are absolutely unique, from which the universal perspectivity of all moral judgments follows as an obvious corollary. Finally, Dewey's desire for continuity led him to an assimilation of moral and factual judgments—an attempt which has already been considered in rather minute detail.

Predominantly critical as this essay has been, it would be a great mistake to conclude that Dewey's philosophy represents merely an *überwundener Standpunkt*, an outmoded fashion which contemporary thought would do well to discard. The truth has rather been, as we have seen, that there is not one Deweyan standpoint but several, and among these there are some which are both original and valuable. Most fruitful has been his conviction that reflective experience is a factor in shaping human life and action and therefore is actually altering in some degree the world we live in; and that philosophy should consequently inquire into the exact character of its rôle. The liberation thus effected in social thinking has been immeasurable; for if thought can modify the natural growth of institutions, the task of the social philosopher is not limited to a description of how society has developed in the past and a forecast of its probable future development, but also implies a measure of responsibility for its evolution towards desired goals. The position of conscious planning has, perhaps, for the first time taken on metaphysical significance in Dewey's philosophy. Guided by this insight he has not hesitated to repudiate the grandiose world-picture of Absolute Idealism, although that philosophy is otherwise congenial to his temperament; and for the otiose security which absolutism gives humanity, he has substituted insecurity with responsibility. His temporalism, which has, in its methodological and metaphysical applications, marked a significant development in contemporary philosophy, was largely derivative from his primary and deep-seated concern with reflective thinking; and it is a pity that other considerations prevented him from developing it to its normal conclusions. In the last chapter his contributions to educational theory which also grew out of the same general interest were discussed at some length.

Much controversy has centered about Dewey's thesis that the personal factor is of decisive importance in all intellectual activity. Although he and many of his followers have frequently made exaggerated claims for this principle, it contains a significant core of truth: that thought is usually motivated by desire, and that constant care is required to safeguard the attainment of impartial conclusions; and, furthermore, that in some (normative) fields of inquiry, it is impossible to obviate the necessity of choice.

Dewey's provisionalism has also, within limits, been a beneficent influence in contemporary thought, especially in social theory and in law. Reflective activity is a hazardous undertaking, and the future success of the rules which are forged from our past experience can never be assured in advance. The most eminent American jurists, Holmes, Pound and Cardozo, have followed out the implications of his logic, and have said with him that general principles are not completely determinative of concrete cases, insisting that if law is to fulfil its function in modern society, legal rules must be employed as working hypotheses, not as final, immutable truths.

Dewey has also been one of the first to take up the task of formulating a revised naturalism—a metaphysics which will do full justice to the qualitative diversity and richness of existence in its immediacies and which, while recognizing the novelties involved in mental phenomena, will bring together in a closer and more intelligible fashion than other theories the physical and mental factors of nature. Although this study has shown that his own treatment of this problem has not been consistent nor his solution of it successful, the problem itself is of prime importance, and any future discussion of it can hardly overlook his work.

And, finally—if a purely personal comment is not out of place in a work of this sort—the writer would like to pay tribute to the stimulating and challenging character of Dewey's writings. He is one of the truly seminal minds in contemporary philosophy, and, if his strength has not lain in analysis, his work, when carefully analyzed, reveals a veritable mine of suggestions and considerations pertinent to the more important philosophical problems. Since philosophy develops through a clarification of its problems, Dewey's place in its history is assured; for an adequate understanding of the considerations which he has brought forward cannot fail to elucidate the nature of these problems.